This exhibition marks the first occasion on which the British Council and The Photographers' Gallery have collaborated on a jointly curated exhibition. This partnership stems from our commitment to promote the work of British-based artists to new audiences beyond our own national borders. Whilst The Photographers' Gallery has consistently exhibited work by emerging and established

ET C GE ART AN

the past twenty years developed an outstanding reputation for the quality and range of its photographic shows, the opportunity to present its newest 'export' in London has rarely been possible. Working in collaboration on every aspect of the exhibition has enabled us to produce a larger and more ambitious project than either partner could have achieved on their own. The overriding motive for undertaking the project was however the realisation that a new generation of British artists, who were pushing the boundaries of photographic practice in new directions, deserved an international platform for their work.

The resulting exhibition, *Reality Check* brings together the work of sixteen artists, some born in Britain, others who have made Britain their home. Whilst not aiming in any way to be a representative survey of current activity, the range and variety of the work included here, by both emerging and more established artists, is united by a shared belief in the camera's capacity to transform real experience into the realm of the poetic. *Reality Check* is an exhibition inspired by real things in the real world — by events, people, relationships, places, things — while moving between differing levels of truth and imagination, perception and pretence. At the beginning of a new century and after a decade of considerable hype about 'Cool Britannia', there would seem to be no better time to take a 'reality check' on the current condition of British photographic and video practice.

Many individuals and organisations have been involved in the realisation of this project. Without the generous support and commitment of the sixteen participating artists and their respective galleries, the exhibition would not have been possible and we would like to extend our appreciation to them for agreeing to lend work for such an extensive tour.

eas venues who have cally involved in the preparation of the show, we remain extremely grateful.

Finally, we would like to pay special thanks to Kate Bush, Senior Programmer at The Photographers' Gallery who has co-curated the exhibition with Brett Rogers, for the vision, commitment and enthusiasm she has brought to all aspects of the project and Alex Farquharson for his perceptive texts. The co-curators are also indebted to Igor Spanjol, Curator of New Media at the Moderna Galerija, Ljubljana who has provided invaluable curatorial input from the outset and to Frédérique Dolivet, Exhibition Assistant at the British Council who has diligently coordinated all aspects of the production of both the catalogue and exhibition.

Paul Wombell
Director
The Photographers' Gallery, London

Brett Rogers
Deputy Director Visual Arts
The British Council

Reality Check
Recent Developments in British
Photography and Video

Kate Bush

'Reality changes, in order
to represent it, modes of
representation must also change.'
[Bertolt Brecht]

Photography, of all the visual
arts, has long been deemed to have
a special relationship with the
real. As a chemically-captured
trace of a world observed it is
unrivalled in its ability to
imitate and describe appearances.
And yet the photograph is not
tautologous with reality: as with
any representation, it is an
abstraction, an image extricated
from the flow of time and the
three dimensions of space.
Photography creates its own
duplicate world, a 'reality in
the second degree', cropped,
framed, and stilled. It occupies
a space permanently in-between the
real and its obverse, pure fantasy
or pure imagination. Realism,
'the real': these terms are
much contested philosophically,
and unsurprisingly photography,
in its documentary form, has been
rendered insecure as their visual
vehicle. In the face of the
critical interrogations of a
generation of post-structuralist
thinkers, it has shied away from
any claims of its sufficiency
to provide a dispassionate,
truthful depiction of the world.

And yet, how do we account for
the proliferation of photography
now? Of 'straight' or observed
photography rather than its
postmodern variant, the found or
appropriated or doctored image? How
do we account for photography
animated by the desire to refer to
a reality that, however problematic
and elusive, nevertheless seems to
have come back to haunt us?
Reality Check is an exhibition
which is inspired by real things
in the real world — by events,
people, relationships, places,
things. And yet it inhabits a
place which is neither purely
experienced nor purely imagined but
hovers somewhere between the two.
Calibrated by differing levels of
truth and imagination, perception
and pretence, *Reality Check* asserts
the potency of the world as a
subject for photography (and its
close relation, video) while
simultaneously exploring the
medium's potential, not as a
mute technology of replication,
but as a discursive artform
rich in poetic possibilities.
A 'reality check', that self-
conscious moment of taking stock,
of gauging the actuality of
something at an instant it
threatens to dissolve into its
opposite — hyperreality, fantasy,
fiction — stands as a metaphor for
the exhibition, and ultimately,
for photography itself.

Dislocated Subjects
Documentary portraiture
conventionally aims to abolish
distance between the subject of
the photograph, and its viewer:
the photographer strives for
closeness or intimacy in order
to reveal something particular
and profound about the subject
in question, probing beyond
physical appearance to capture
the psychological core of the
individual, in the expectation
that this emotional empathy
is communicable to any number
of subsequent viewers.
The establishment of empathy
towards the subject in the mind
of the viewer is triggered by any
number of devices: by picturing
the subject at an intensely
private moment, by having them
gaze directly into the camera,
by forcing them to stand as
representatives of universal human
emotions — passion, despondency,
ecstasy — or by the simple act of
naming them. This is the strategy
that underpins the humanist
portraiture of photographers like
Nan Goldin and Annelies Štrba.
Conversely, for a number of artists
in *Reality Check*, portraiture can
act to shut down the possibility
of empathy in order to provoke a

more complex range of responses from the viewer. In the work of Shizuka Yokomizo, Bettina von Zwehl and Lesley Shearer, an intense transaction occurs between photographer and subject, but one which doesn't encourage intimacy or proximity, and instead stresses difference or distance.

Take Shizuka Yokomizo's *Stranger* series (1999-2001). She writes a letter to someone she has never met, but whom she knows to live on the ground floor of a house or apartment somewhere in the city. The letter is addressed simply to "Dear Stranger" – and signed, equally anonymously, "From The Artist". The letter states that at a particular time and date, Yokomizo will be waiting with her camera outside their window and will, if they choose to co-operate, take their portrait as they draw their curtains and look outside towards her. They, the subjects, are promised a copy of their image at the conclusion of the exercise, but the artist requests that the contract of anonymity is never breached and they will never attempt to make contact with her again.

The stranger — whether oppressed outsider, exotic foreigner or elusive celebrity — is the stock subject of traditional documentary, but here the 'strangeness' of the stranger is concentrated *in extremis*, rather than struggled to be overcome through a state of temporary intimacy willed by the photographer towards the photographed. Most photographed people present themselves to the lens of the camera rather than the person behind it, and yet here, it is the photographer, crouching behind her apparatus in the obscurity of the night, who is as much the undiscovered subject of the picture, as each individual peers out at the mysterious voyeur. In these portraits, photographer and subject are both looking, and being looked at: both are active subjects of their gaze, and, simultaneously, passive objects of the gaze of the Other. Intimacy, and its correlative, empathy, are replaced with a more varied emotional register – wariness, fear, curiosity, trepidation, anxiety, hesitation. You are aware that these are real pictures, of real people, and yet you are also aware that the event is self-consciously stage-managed (by the photographer) and self-consciously performed (by the subjects). Like a piece of Brechtian theatre, the mechanism of the production of the image is

laid bare in front of the viewer (in the form of the original letter), in order to short-circuit our illusory identification with the people in the portraits. Operating around a two-way dynamic of calculated estrangement, *Stranger* could be described as a dramatised photography of 'otherness'.

Bettina von Zwehl's meticulously realised portraits also centre around manipulated subjects in order to simultaneously summon and subvert a sense of the real. With their reduced palettes, restrained vocabulary of pose and gesture, and hard, clear profiles, these portraits are highly aestheticised, a strategy which joined to von Zwehl's air of cool scientific scrutiny, imposes a deliberate level of detachment between subject and viewer. In a trilogy of portrait sequences dating from 1998 to 1999, von Zwehl, rather like a scientist conducting a controlled experiment, subjected groups of sitters to three types of physiological manipulation before photographing them: she forced them to wake up in the middle of the night, to overexert themselves in a hot room, to hold their breath lying on the floor in total darkness. The subjects stare intently into the camera. Rather like Thomas Ruff's hugely enlarged 'passport' pictures, they reveal everything of their physiognomy and nothing of their psychology. Yet unlike Ruff, they do not appear as simulated human beings, as empty photographic doubles. These people flush and sweat, they struggle to focus their eyes, their bodies yield to the pressure of gravity: they are sentient, conscious beings, even if their experience as subjects has been manufactured by the artist. Von Zwehl's deterministic approach isolates and exaggerates something that perhaps lies at the heart of all photographic portraiture: that there's no such thing as an objective depiction of a real human being, only varying degrees of influence and control on the part of the photographer in the imaging of identity.

In Lesley Shearer's *Falling* (2001–02) there is a comparable insistence on the body, rather than the brain, as the locus of a subject dislocated from themselves, and thus from the viewer. A tattoo here, a badly fitting dress there, clammy skin or a fold of flesh, these are the only marks of individual identity left in a scenario where her subjects – induced by liberal amounts of alcohol and the hot blaze of

photographic lamps — have abandoned any sense of self-composure, withdrawn their gaze, and fallen into an oblivious, almost catatonic, state. As this slippage of consciousness occurs, Shearer photographs them. The retreat from consciousness is mirrored in their retreat from the frame of the photograph. They appear off-centre, cramped within or literally falling out of pictorial space: a formal metaphor to describe a regressive, psychological moment. These dark, sinking, romantic portraits promise a delving into the interior being, but they do not deliver and you are left firmly shut out of the subjects' inner worlds.

The figuring of uncomfortable subjects as a way of disrupting the normative process of identification that occurs between viewer and photographic subject, is taken to a different extreme in the video work of k r buxey and Michelle Williams. Both artists put themselves centrally in the picture. Both perform scenarios which, drawing on morbid or aggressive eroticism, make for uneasy viewing. Michelle Williams' *Sunday Afternoon II* (2001) is bathed in the lush colour of a post-war movie and slowed in tempo. A figure lies prone on the floor in a living-room while two dogs, made giant by the ground-level view, insistently lap at her body with their impossibly long, wet tongues. Lifeless or acquiescent? Corpse or lover? The scene is ambiguous in its cause, unambiguous in its effect: a disquieting conjunction of death and bestial eroticism.

k r buxey's work is defiantly hardcore and, quite literally, in your face. Despite being conspicuously staged and stylised, pornography trades in a belief in the reality of bodies: it exists, for its consumers, on both a phantasmatic and physiological level. k r buxey exploits this contradiction, this suturing of truth and fiction, in her performed parodies of pornographic scenarios. *Such A Feeling's Coming Over Me* (2001), in which she restages directly to camera a 'bukkake' scene (a Japanese porn genre in which hordes of men ejaculate on the face of a single woman) renders a scene of female humiliation and violation confusingly comical. With an encouraging smile and an effervescent style — and set to the wholesome voice of Karen Carpenter — k r buxey, covered in cum, makes ridiculous porn's endless repetitions of orgasmic pleasure. *negrophilia — A ROMANCE* (2001)

confronts head-on two unspoken sexual tropes: rampant black male sexuality, and the predatory, sexually autonomous, white woman. It's an autobiographical 'love story', written, spoken, directed, and filmed by the artist, and starring herself and an ex-lover. Its x-rated narrative, a pornographic paean to the superiority of black sexual anatomy, accompanies visual fragments of the body in question, interlaced with images of the two having, and completing, sex. No longer the submissive object of *Such A Feeling's Coming Over Me*, k r buxey is here aggressively in charge and on top. And yet her sexual emancipation comes at the cost of another's objectification and violation: sexist stereotypes are dislodged by racist ones. Despite their egregious approach, k r buxey's videos represent a nuanced excavation of sexual politics and the pornographic imagination.

Painting the Everyday
British art has always opted for observable fact and personal experience over metaphysical adventures or idealistic manifestos. "England", declared Nikolaus Pevsner in 1956, "has never been happy with the Grand Manner." Joshua Reynolds, founder of the Royal Academy, Britain's first art school in 1778, saw no contradiction in exhorting the artists of the day to devote themselves to grand themes and epic histories while he himself pursued the lowlier genre of portraiture. Quintessentially British artists like Hogarth, Gainsborough, Constable and the pre-Raphaelites, understood how to transmute the everyday into high art: they worked outwards from the individual and the particular to the universal. Photography has always been better placed than painting "to extract a difference from the repetition of the everyday" (Deleuze). Indeed, photography might claim to be the Art of the Everyday, so it is unsurprising that British photographers, in a tradition stemming from Fox Talbot to Richard Billingham, have displayed a preference for a visual empiricism rooted in the world immediately around them.

Nigel Shafran's *Washing-Up 2000* can be considered in the light of this tradition. It's a work which takes the most unpromising subject imaginable and creates from it a series of luminous still lifes which veneer poetry onto the surfaces of the everyday. Comprising over 170 images made during the course of a year, the series documents a corner of Shafran's kitchen with the washing-up done and drying in the aftermath of a meal. Far from summoning the deadening repetitions of quotidian life, it marks instead a sense of reassuring ritual and the evenness of time passing. There is smallness and ordinariness here, but also a richness of experience: each glass, each plate seems coated with the memories of meals shared, conversations had, intimacies enjoyed. As with all diaries, it historicises the everyday, lending it weight and meaning. Shafran's intuitive feeling for the substantiality of commonplace objects, his simple vision of the washing-up as a constantly evolving, involuntary sculpture, where "the shapes keep changing", accounts for the compositional harmony of his images. That, and a Chardin-esque sensitivity to the effect of light playing off objects — though here, the utensils are wrought from bright plastics and stainless metals — elevates the commonplace into the realm of pictorial beauty. His new series, of charity shop interiors and street markets, also deals with the passage of time and the stuff of everyday life. In each of these display spaces, different temporalities exist side-by-side in the form of piles of objects — the latest luxury version alongside last year's model, things long out of fashion, and things that never quite made it in — displayed for consumption once more. The charity shop symptomises a post-Thatcherite economic decline but also, perhaps, a British antipathy towards the obsolescence of things: here, value is never permanently lost, merely endlessly recycled.

A similar ecology of the everyday underpins Ori Gersht's sequence of 1950s English school buildings, long past their sell-by date but still very much in use. This architecture epitomises the will of post-war governments to provide education-for-all in rebuilt schools following the devastation of the Blitz — but as so often in England, it resulted in utopianism on the cheap, driven as much by frugality as ideology. With their modular structures and their flat façades built from planes of glass, concrete and bright primary colour, these schools adapted the language of architectural Modernism, within what were essentially frail and provisional structures. Gersht's panoramic photographs — taken frontally and spreading horizontally — emphasise surface,

flatness, monochromacity and the serial, grid-like basis of the buildings' construction: all characteristics, of course, of Modernist painting. But rather than symbolising some bright new future, these buildings speak of gradual decay, their colours fading and the concrete dampening. Modernism's vision of an art purged of all vulgar concerns with reality, is here brought into tension with the actualities of life: in Gersht's photographs, ideal aestheticism collides with a rougher reality.

Like Nigel Shafran and Ori Gersht, Dryden Goodwin is an artist who marries a painterly sensibility to what is, at root, a photography — albeit a moving photography — of the everyday. Goodwin typically treats the media of video and sound as malleable materials akin to paint and canvas: as elements which can be fragmented into their constituent parts — of individual notes and single frames — and then recomposed into luminous, symphonic compositions. His latest work *Closer* (2002), a video triptych with sound, makes explicit this relationship between the gestural activity of painting and the photographed image. Moving from edge to centre of a nocturnal city, with a long-distance laser pen in one hand and a video camera in the other, Goodwin trains the red laser onto first the cityscape, then the façades of individual buildings, and finally, the bodies of strangers viewed through windows from a dark street. The hot, burning light lingers on a back, a face, a hand, as it touches the skin or traces the profile of an unsuspecting individual. In *Closer*, 'drawing' is treated as both a noun — a linear or schematic representation — and a verb — the process of pulling, or being pulled closer, towards something. In addition to this sense of increasing proximity, the red light also works to 'draw out', or to prolong, a fleeting encounter which might otherwise disappear into the bustling flux and anonymity of urban life. In *Closer*, those momentary gestures and passing glances that play out between people in the space of the city are beautifully paralleled in Goodwin's 'drawing with light'. Sometimes intrusive, sometimes caressing, the touch of the light illuminates that strange mix of intimacy and anonymity, closeness and distance, which characterises human exchange within urban space.

David Shrigley also makes fugitive interventions directly within the landscape. His interventions mostly take the form of drawn or written signs which helpfully annotate bits of the world most of us would walk past. Where the Situationists before him saw the city as a huge canvas, ripe with potential for mass expression and interpretation, Shrigley's much more modest brand of psycho-geography maps meaning and possibility in the smallest of phenomena: a hole in the fence, a fallen tree, a forgotten Filofax. A sense of civic responsibility fuels *Ignore This Building* (1998), with its little handscrawled petition a lonely voice of dissent in the face of the eternally bombastic ambitions of urban planners. This sense of social conscience can take a rather nasty turn however, like the booby-trapped frisbee lying in wait for unsuspecting kiddies in a playground (*Landmine*, 1995), or the local newsagent's cruelly public proclamation that *Brian is a Twat* (1998). At times, a note of irony gets the upper hand, as he strings a coconut from a goalpost and exhorts local footballers to *Try to be Happy* (1997) while they kick the ball across the wasteground of a depressed city.

Fabulous Realism

Built environments are also a recurring theme in the work of Luke Gottelier and Saskia Olde Wolbers. Theirs is not an architecture of heroic monuments or triumphal edifices but one assembled from various spent and discarded materials that crowd the everyday, to become architectures of the imagination, built up from real things into spaces of fabulous invention.

Luke Gottelier's lo-fi photographs tread a daring line between inchoate nothingness and eccentric imagination. Working with dishevelled, almost formless materials — a dollop of custard, a manky carpet, a length of unruly masking tape or a skein of string — his images, depending on how you look at them, remain exactly what they are — or else propel you to an entirely different place. The elements are pure grunge in the baseness of their materiality, and yet this trash is invested with a sense of poetic possibility. Drizzles of custard evolve, in his imagination, into a view *Under a Table* (2001), or a *Man Looks at Telegraph Poles* (2001); or simply, *An Arch* (2001). A tangle of tape and another splodge of viscous liquid is *The Debating Society* (2000). Miscellaneous office items, a nail brush and some twigs become *An Obelisk* (1999). It's the

antithesis of the hyperreal constructs made by artists such as Thomas Demand or James Casebere, where the camera tricks the eye into believing the veracity of the setting. In Gottelier's world the camera doesn't 'make real', but, with its bright auras and dark shadows, its fogs and veils of light, it casts further levels of metaphysical uncertainty over the scene, while opening up a space for our own imaginations.

Saskia Olde Wolbers' futuristic architectures might look like computer-created fantasies, but in fact they are entirely real — handcrafted and shot in her studio. These scenes form the visual complement to a series of narrated tales, all of which have their basis in life. "Let's in our heads go forward to the year 2016, the year in which I will be conceived. So begins *Kilowatt Dynasty* (2000), an extravagant story which involves a young Chinese girl, a huge dam, a teleshopping empire, a washing machine, and a vast subterranean world. The narrator recounts the tale of her future conception, an event which arises from her father, an environmental activist who spends years handcuffed to a fence in a bid to stop the dam, kidnapping her mother, teleshopping TV presenter and wearer of a "tangerine coloured two-piece". As the unborn child talks, the camera floats over a breathtakingly strange, oneiric world; a shimmering mindscape of viscous liquids and translucent architectural forms. We could be in the womb with the unborn foetus, underwater in a marine nature documentary, or someplace — as you notice that this liquid world looks suspiciously like the inside of a plastic water bottle — altogether more ordinary.

Olde Wolbers' narrative videos are prompted by tales of human drama read in the newspapers or heard on the radio. Mandy Ellwood, for example, a British woman who became pregnant with octuplets and notoriously sold her story to the tabloids, inspired the lead character in *Octet* (1997); the building of the Three Gorges Dam and the imminent flooding of an entire province in China, sets the scene for *Kilowatt Dynasty*. Onto these real-life events, Olde Wolbers embroiders fantastic, rambling stories, told in the form of an off-camera voiceover. Her protagonists hatch ambitiously creative schemes which tend to go horribly wrong: like poor Luis Zarzuela, the star of *Day-Glo* (1999), an uxurious Andalusian market gardener, who in a bid to make a fast buck creates a virtual reality theme park only to discover his beloved wife is committing adultery — with a virtual version of his younger self. Olde Wolbers' characters become victims of their own excessive imaginations who end up unable to distinguish their dreams from reality. Her stories of individual calamity are contemporary parables which warn of the deleterious impact of technological interventions — from reproductive science to virtual entertainment — on humanity and sense, in an increasingly technology-driven world.

Alan Currall is another teller of tall stories. Typically featuring himself delivering a deadpan monologue to camera, his works are the video diaries of someone attempting to answer life's more awkward existential questions. Not naturally comfortable in front of the camera, Currall's faltering delivery convinces us of the authenticity of his accounts — only for us to discover that this ostensibly ordinary life masks a wild imagination and, possibly, a superhuman existence. In *Jetsam* (1995), he reveals himself to be, not a struggling artist from Glasgow but a shape-shifting alien who, accidentally crash-landed in central Scotland, is biding his time while his companions work to repair their ship at a local vehicle repair shop. In *Message To My Best Friend* (2000), what seems to be a heartfelt tribute to his best mate, turns first to embarrassing sycophancy and then, a worrying level of obsession. It is an old truism that appearances can be deceptive, and in Currall's world, nothing is quite as certain as it first appears.

Politics personified

Photographers who engage directly with the world and its political problems are traditionally gathered under the rubric of 'social documentary'. Political and social complexities are addressed in this exhibition, but not in the form of simple realism or illustrative documentary: for few now hold faith in the power of photography to exert real political change. Instead, an artist like Phil Collins works against the grain of the documentary canon in order to question the integrity of its representations — at the same time accepting that the photographic image, without guaranteeing truth, might still ease understanding of political realities. Collins mimics the codes and conventions of

mainstream conflict reportage (the video interview, the anti-aesthetic photograph), in his work based in trouble spots around the world: Northern Ireland, the Balkans, post-September 11th New York, and, in progress — Baghdad. Where most social documentary, inevitably if not intentionally, turns one person's plight into another's passing entertainment, Collins' work resists the spectacularisation of other lives into visual theatre. And where most social documentary operates under a mask of supposedly dispassionate observation, Collins is open about the way his camera manipulates the subsequent presentation of events. Whether photographing refugees in a Macedonian camp, Belfast teenagers or young Serbs in post-war Belgrade, Collins finds individuals, not ciphers of political tragedy. He asks them intimate, sometimes banal questions: Where's your father? What shampoo do you use? Where's a good place to fall in love? He photographs them at emotionally significant moments — Sanja, the moment her boyfriend leaves for the Serbian army, Igor, beaten up during the first Belgrade Pride March, Vanja, who's trying to give up smoking — to reveal them as individuals with their own feelings, desires, flaws and confusions. This is social documentary in which the personal is not subsumed to, but becomes, the political.

Graham Fagen also brings art to bear on contemporary social and political issues but rather than pursuing a documentary language, he refracts these subjects through the prism of older cultural forms such as classical theatre, the novel and allegorical painting. Where previous work has dealt with subjects of conflict and class, in *Reality Check* he contributes a series of enigmatic photographic portraits which draw on the anachronistic form of allegory. These portraits personify cultural forces — broadcasting, education, the arts, myth — in the shape of human figures. Fagen supplies their biographies — the *Owner of Broadcasting* (2000–01) is the youngest (born in 1901), the *Owner of Education* (2000–01) probably the oldest (born in Africa, date unknown, possibly during the Palaeolithic or Neolithic periods). The cultural 'forces' are, in the language of capitalism, 'owned' by each individual. Education, for example, is not presented as an abstract, civilising power, but as a person with something to sell: "Her methods and their aims change depending on the needs of the

people she sold her practice to (…)
Working relationships with religion
and more recently, governments,
have helped her to establish formal
institutions of education." Myth,
"originally one of the good people
of Greece, many of who went on to
become known as 'gods'. She took a
different path however, realising
the potential of selling her truth
and knowledge in order to help
control the universe and to make
mankind's activities in it
efficacious." Fagen's *Owners*
allegorise the fact that the
supposedly neutral values of
Western civilisation are never in
themselves innocent of, or
impervious to, bigger political
forces: knowledge, after all,
is power, and has been, and is,
consistently used and abused.

Reality Checked

Where photography, in Graham
Fagen's hands, works to release
a truth hidden behind the surface
of the picture, Keith Tyson is
interested only in manifest,
not latent content. His series of
Expanded Repeaters could claim to
be the most purely documentary
works in *Reality Check*. They have
no artistic or semantic ambition
beyond a desire to provide the most
accurate visual record possible of
their chosen subject. And yet they
couldn't look more different to a
documentary photograph. And their
subjects, being mostly invisible,
couldn't be more antithetical to
the standard photographic
repertoire of people, places and
things. These subjects are
precisely defined — one degree
Celsius of temperature, 60 seconds
of time, one metre of movement
along a one-dimensional axis — and
even more precisely represented.
The *Expanded Repeaters* are mindful
of the philosophical conundrum
that, while 'the real' has no
'edges', no beginning or end, no
decisive moment, the 'photograph'
does. Thus, in the interests of a
more accurate rendition of reality,
they eschew the photograph
understood as a singular image,
or one discrete moment, and propose
it instead as a complex
representation of the dynamic
intervals between measurable
things. The *Expanded Repeaters*
are typically bi-sided, aggregative
assemblages, which appear exactly
replicated on right and left hand
sides. But look very closely and
you see that they are not: minute
variations occur across each set
of paired elements within the
whole. It is here, in this
perceptual doubletake, in the
space between seemingly identical
but measurably different things,
that reality is checked out.

If Keith Tyson's *Expanded
Repeaters* describe a space that is
empirically sound, then Roderick
Buchanan's *Catch 60'6"* (2001)
renders space empirically suspect.
In this video installation, you
believe you are audience to a
baseball game between two players,
as a ball appears to whistle at
regular intervals across a large
distance — in fact, the exact
distance between pitcher and batter
on a real field. It appears that
the two players caught on video
are lobbing, then catching,
then lobbing the ball back and
forth between each other. In fact
it is a game of illusion, where the
passage of the ball is apprehended
subliminally in our minds, rather
than actually witnessed, and where
the two players, individually
engaged in a practice session,
play not each other but themselves
The piece is staged with split-
second accuracy to sustain the
illusion. It charts a gap between
belief and experience — between
what you think is there, and what
actually is — to take its own very
particular reality check.

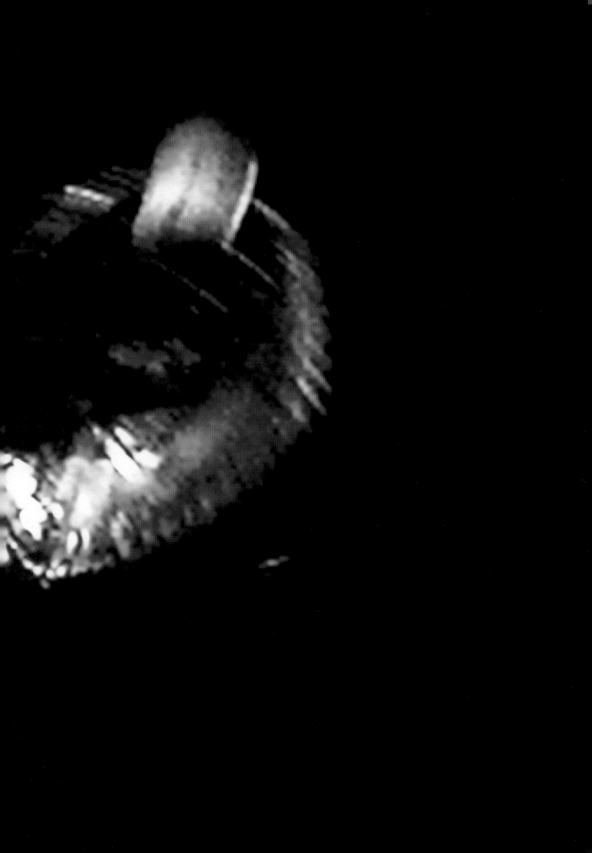

Phil Collins
Milan and Vesna, not on tramadol
from the series *Becoming More
Like Us* 2002
lambda print
61 x 91 cm

20— **Phil Collins**
21 *Post-op 1, Institute of Oncology,*
   Belgrade from the series
   Becoming More Like Us 2002
   lambda print
   61 x 91 cm

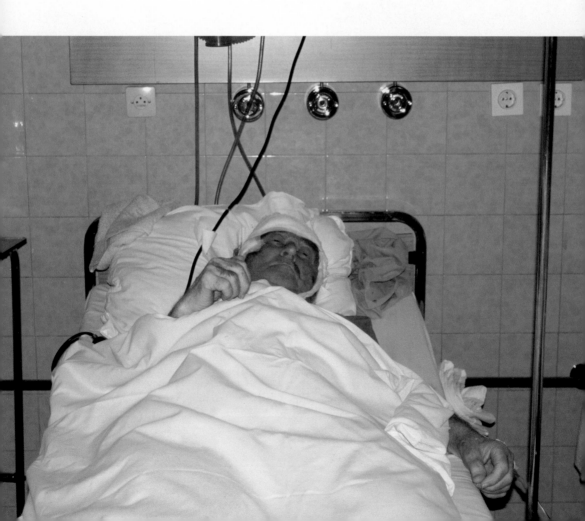

Phil Collins
*The Best Postie in Belgrade,
as awarded by the Mayor* from
the series *Becoming More
Like Us* 2002
lambda print
61 x 91 cm

Phil Collins
Siniša and Sanja after the funeral
from the series *Becoming More Like
Us* 2001
lambda print
122 x 149

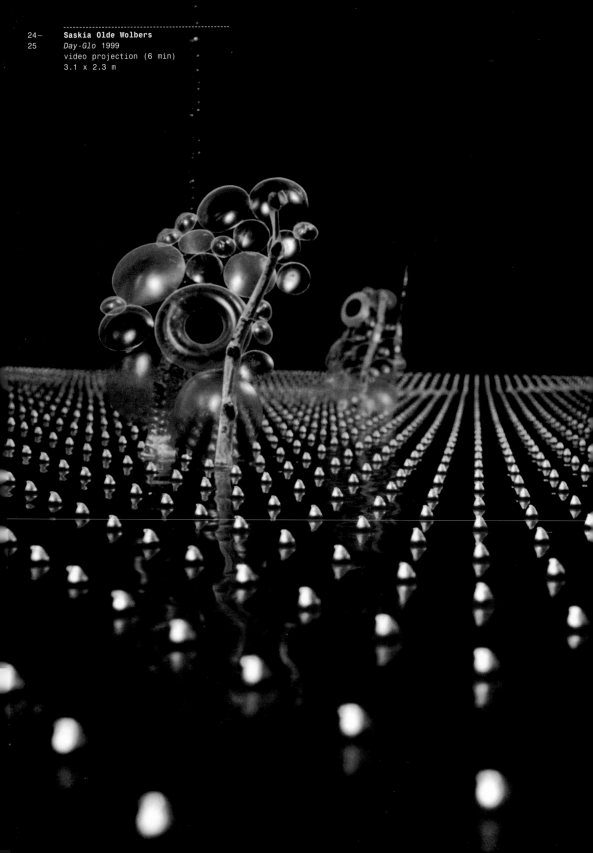

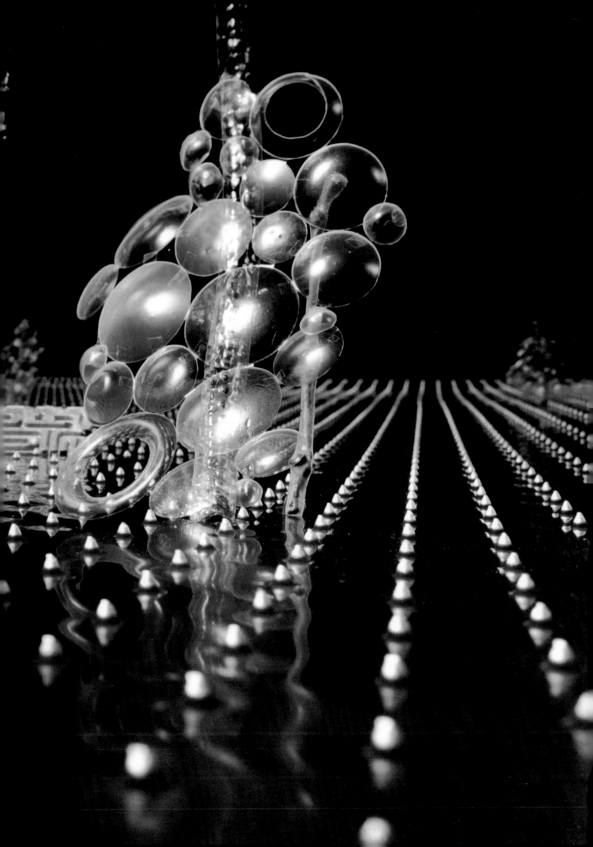

Saskia Olde Wolbers
Kilowatt Dynasty 2000
video projection (7 min)
3 x 4 m

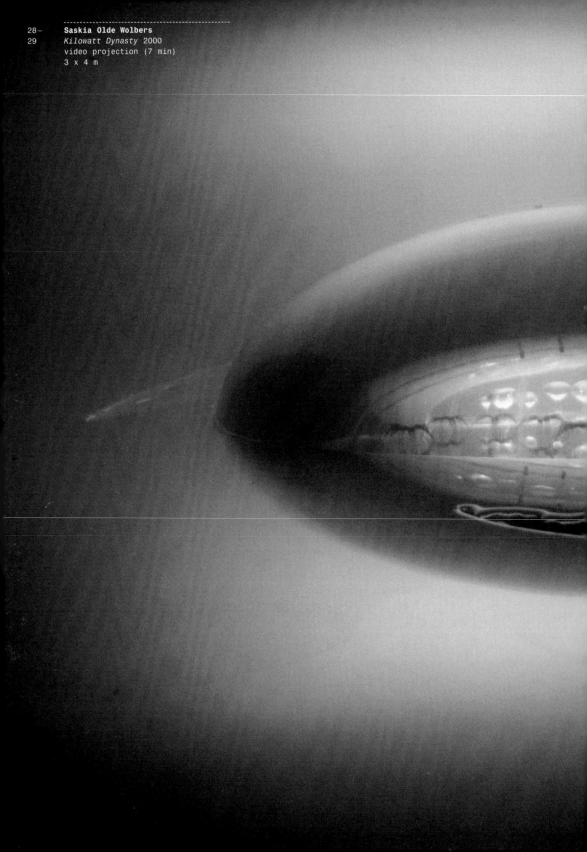

Saskia Olde Wolbers
Kilowatt Dynasty 2000
video projection (7 min)
3 x 4 m

Shizuka Yokomizo
Stranger 1999–2001
c-type prints
108 x 127 cm (80 x 80 cm image)

36—
37

Alan Currall

Message To My Best Friend 2000
video on monitor (4 min)

I know it's really embarrassing,
but I just wanted to tell you that
you're my best friend.

    You … you always have been and
probably always will be … my best
friend. I can't imagine anyone ever
being as important to me as you
are. You're … you're always there
for me when I need someone to talk
to … about anything. You're always
willing to listen … never turn me
away or give me a cold shoulder.
You're, … you're always warm and
open towards me. You make me laugh.
You always make me happy to be
around you. There's … there's no
one who ever gives me better advice
than you. I've probably known you
for longer than I've known anyone
else. And in all that time … well …
we've never fallen out … not in any
big way. And … you're just so
compassionate and … sensitive …
that I don't feel that there's
anything I can't talk to you about.
You've got … a great record
collection and … the way you dress
is really kind of cool but funky
and … never following any set
fashions or trends … but always
striking out in your own direction
… and others follow. You're always
surrounded by the coolest people
and sometimes when un-cool people
hang around with you, you always
manage to shake them off with your
rapier wit. You're kind of good
looking and … just … you even smell
good. Sometimes I wonder why I
bother with anyone else, because …
no one would ever match up to you.
And I just wanted to take this time
out to thank you for being such a …
great person.

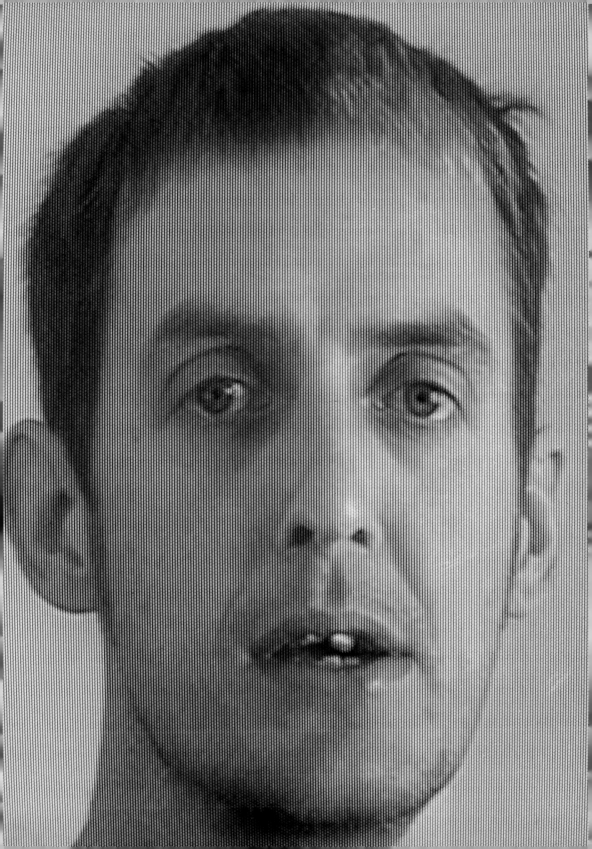

38–   **Alan Currall**
39   *Jetsam* 1995
        video on monitor (4 min)

Well, we were flying over central Scotland, and we got buzzed by a couple of airforce jets and we had to make a crash landing. And we came down just east of Stirling — no, just west of Stirling. And we had to abandon the ship because we thought it was going to blow, for a while. It didn't, and we hid it. We've got it under a cloaking device now and well, we made our way to, well I came to Glasgow. There was five of us on board. We've all got various jobs and things now. Well actually no (one of us is on the dole). I decided to be an artist, because I'd always been good at drawing, and I got a job one day a week at the art school, and that's good because I get to meet a lot of people from all over, it's quite cosmopolitan and it's interesting. We had to … fortunately we go polymorphous, and we can change our shape to whatever we want to. We thought it best to go human because there seemed to be more of them, and they're least likely to notice us. I decided to be English because I wasn't very good at the Scottish accent. Looking forward to getting back home. Two of the crew are now working at a vehicle repair shop and they're picking up bits and pieces with which we eventually hope to get the ship back and running again. Maybe by the end of the year. I'll miss it here. Yeah I shall miss it. Had quite a bit of success with the art lately, and it's nothing that would really go down well back on my planet. So I'll have to abandon all that, and I'm quite enjoying it. But of course I miss home and it's quite a good job I've got anyway, like, flying flying-saucers.

That's about it really. Okay?

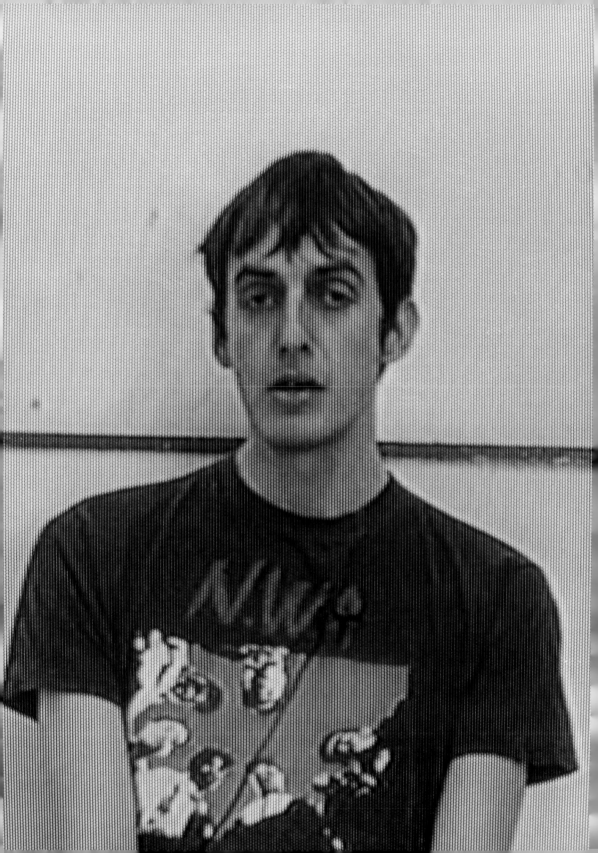

Alan Currall
Pretending To Live In A
Safer World 2001
video on monitor (12 min)

Ori Gersht
Knowledge Factories 1999–2001
c-type prints
50 x 100 cm

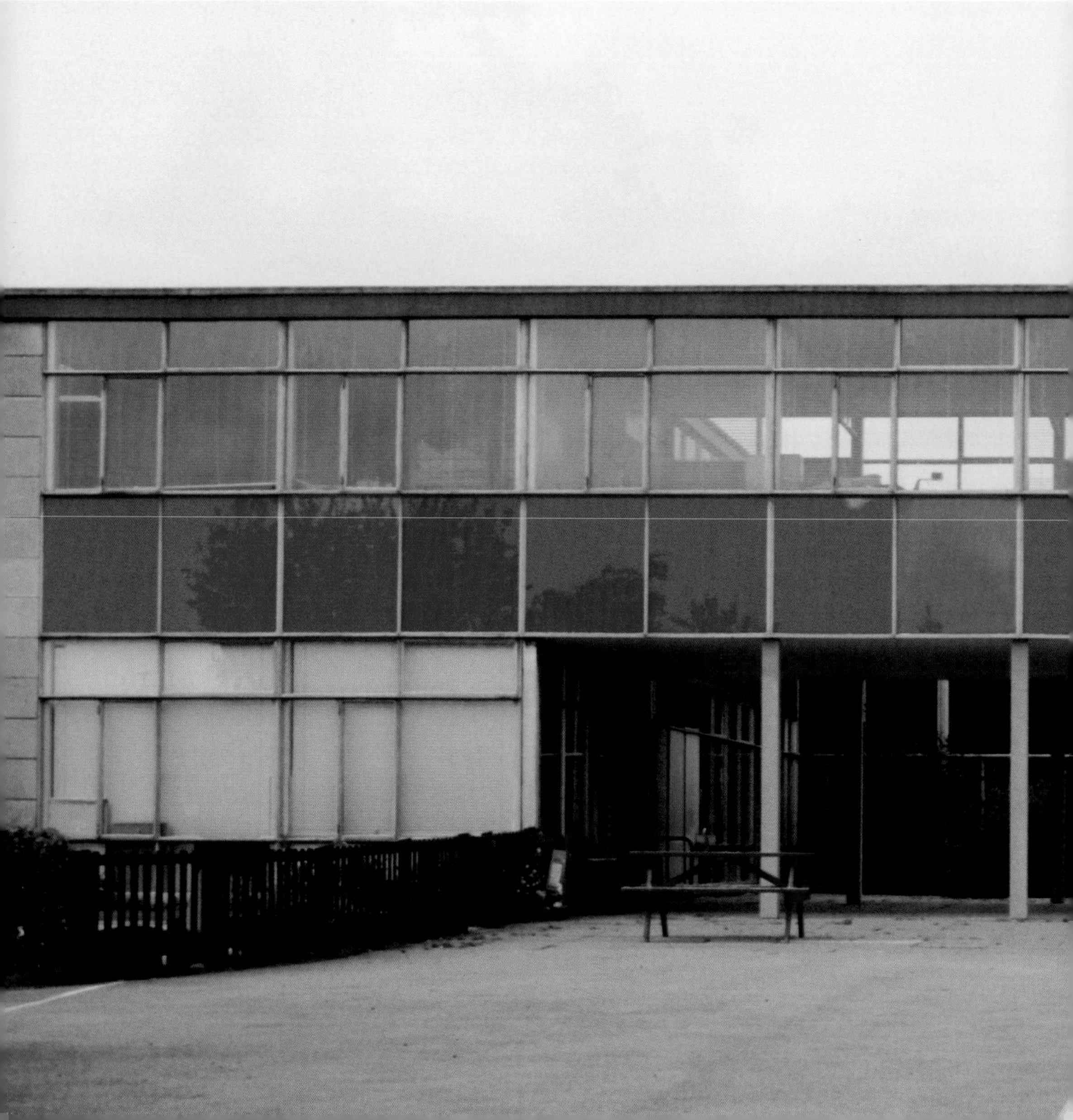

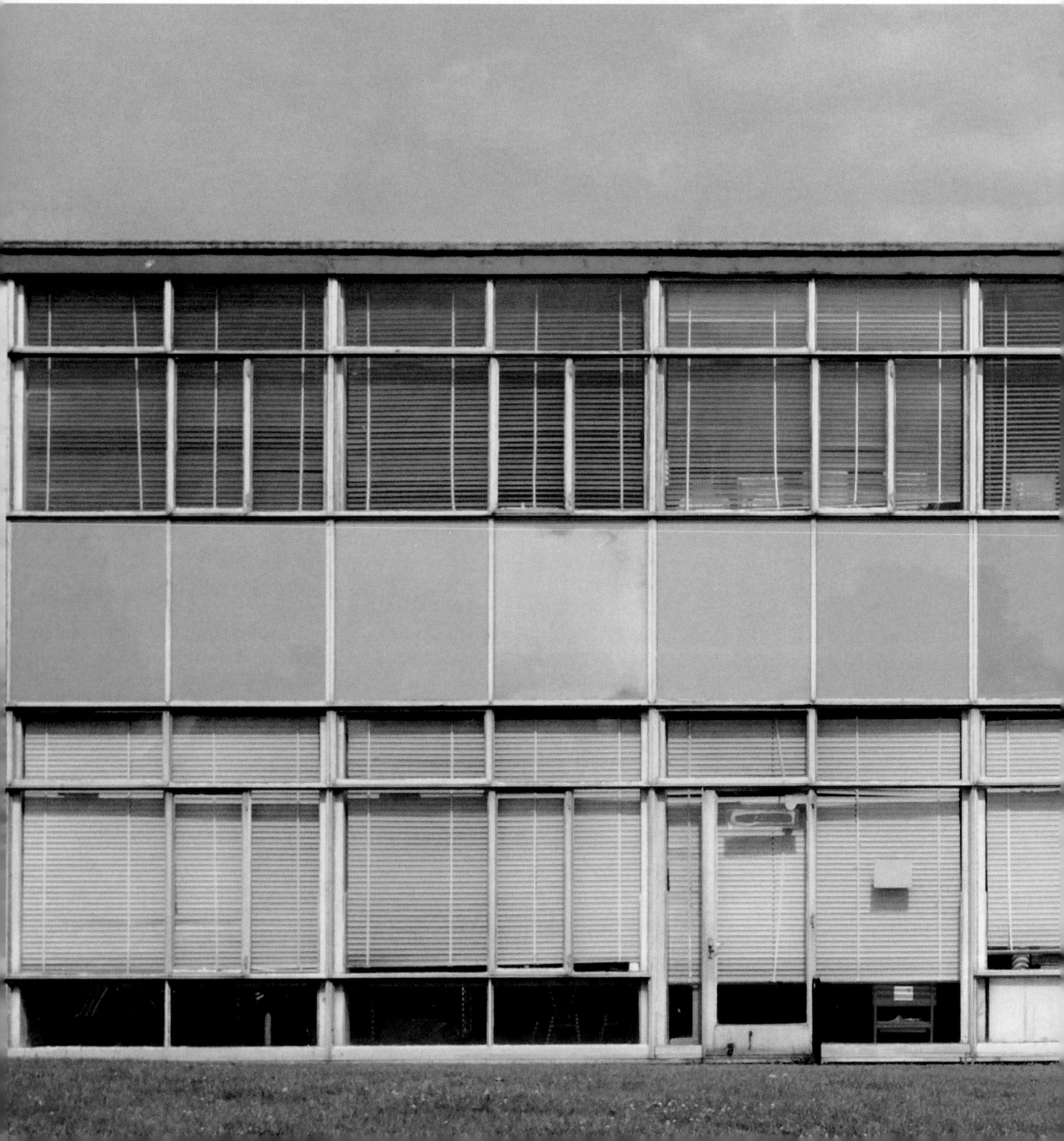

Luke Gottelier
Man Looks at Telegraph Poles 2001
colour photograph
81 x 122 cm

Luke Gottelier
An Obelisk 1999
colour photograph
81 x 122 cm

Nigel Shafran
Stuff 2002
c-type print
47 x 60 cm

Nigel Shafran
Washing-Up 2000
c-type prints
47 x 60 cm

---

25 April 2000
   8.00pm by Terry's watch.
Branflakes toast milk tea at John
and Sara's in Glasgow (eaten on
motorway) chicken Dalgleish,
potatoes and veg, strawberry and
apple sponge with cream at Jill &
Terrys with Jo, Kathy and Ruth.

---

20 May 2000
   Ruth and me, caffe latte and
shared a croissant on Hudson St,
Chicken wrap for lunch B&Q with
PIR and H in New Haven, Salmon,
halibut, chicken, steak sweetcorn,
potatoe salad, courgettes and
mushrooms.

4 February 2000
   Ruth away, didn't wash up last night, herbal tea with Mickey, Japanese restaurant.

16 March 2000
   1.30pm 2nd photograph of the day. Breakfast crumpets and tea, (mine with cottage cheese and honey, Ruth's with Marmite) with Jose and Claudio (who I think washed up).

k r buxey
negrophilia – A ROMANCE 2001
video on monitor (10 min)

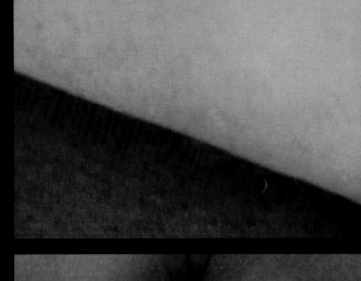

Baby's dick splits Comfort,
Featherlite, Extra-Safe, Gossamer
and Avanti.

Baby,
says i—
we need to get you
big-black-African-man condoms
for that
big-black-African-man-dick

i am
"a good fit" which
makes us
happy.

Baby says that someone must have put
a curse on me
to make me want this Big Black Dick
between my legs.

Baby says i am "frosty"
he says I speak to him "in a funny
way"
he says I am just a "typical
English girl"
which
I am

Baby says he is
leaving

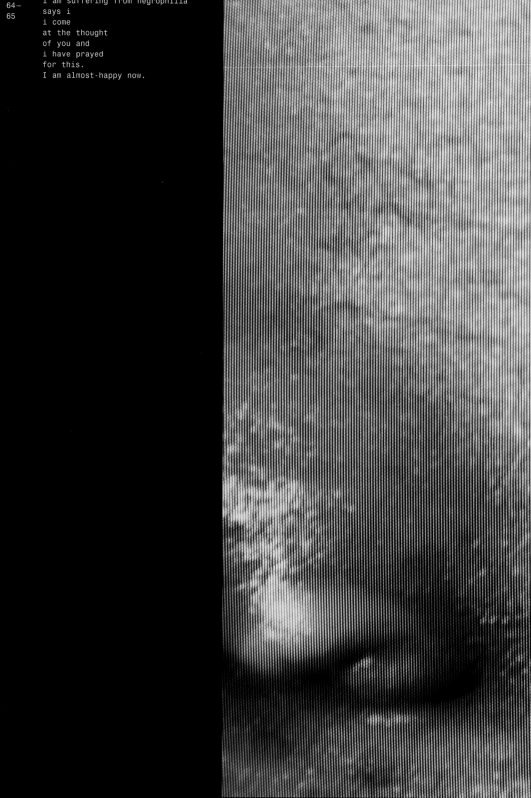

i am suffering from negrophilia
says i
i come
at the thought
of you and
i have prayed
for this.
I am almost-happy now.

Bettina von Zwehl
from the series *Untitled II* 1999
c-type prints
120 x 90 cm

68–71
from the series *Profiles*
Diptych #4 and *Diptych #3* 2001
c-type prints
84 x 63 cm each panel

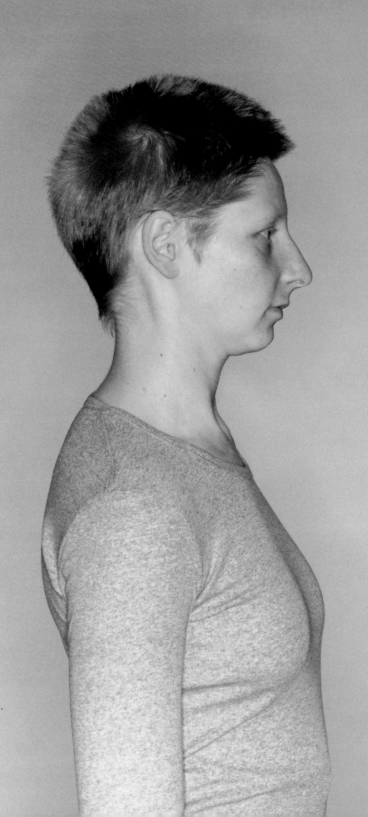

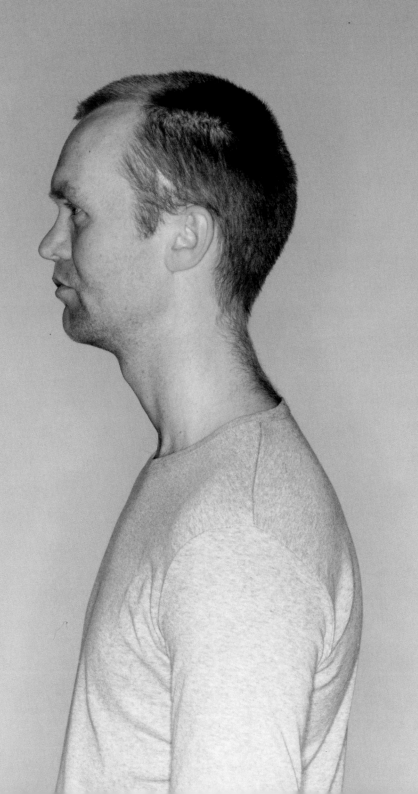

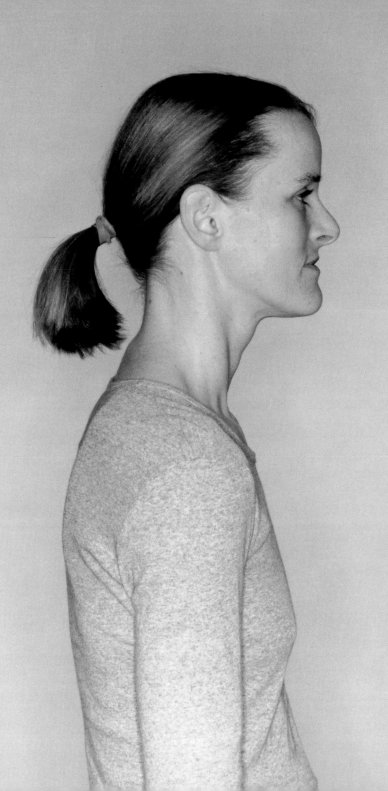

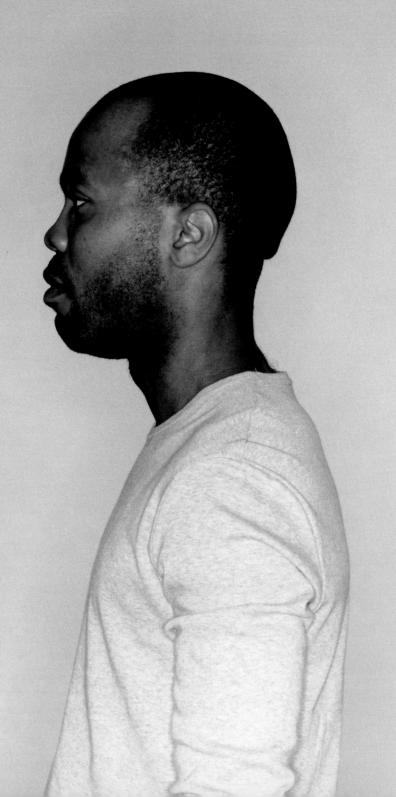

Michelle Williams
Sunday Afternoon II 2001
video projection
(6 min 28 sec)
dimensions variable

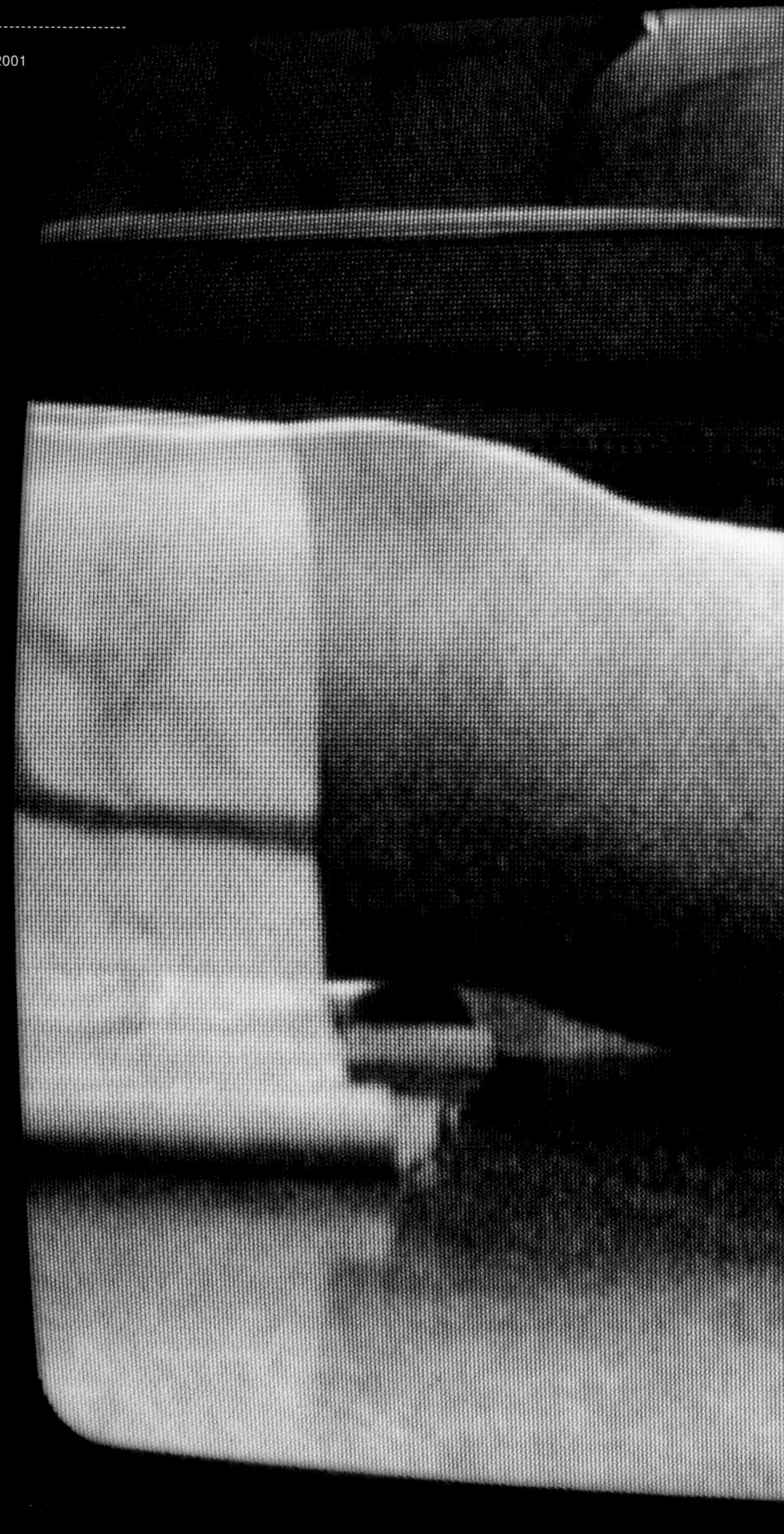

Lesley Shearer
from the series *Falling* 2001–02
digital photograph from Polaroid
106 x 137 cm

80–   **Lesley Shearer**
81   from the series *Falling* 2001–02
       digital photographs from Polaroid
       137 x 106 cm

85—   **Keith Tyson**
        A Universal Cooling within the
        Everyday Photographic Array
        (detail) 2000-01
        mixed media installation
        dimensions variable
        Collection of
        Poju & Anita Zabludowicz

88–
89

Keith Tyson
Dual Workstations (30 seconds late and early) 1998–99 from the series *Artmachine Repeater*
mixed media installation
dimensions variable
Collection of Norman and Norah Stone, San Francisco
Courtesy Thea Westreich Art Advisory Services, New York

90—
91

David Shrigley

Untitled (Welcome, Failte, Bienvenue, Bienvenido, Bienvenuto, Wilkommen) 1999
c-type print
30.5 x 30.5 cm

The Ship 1992
c-type print
30 x 30 cm

David Shrigley
Brian is a twat 1998
c-type print
25.3 x 25.4 cm

*Untitled (This H stands for
Hello Welcome to the Park)* 1999
c-type print
30.5 x 30.5 cm

David Shrigley
Your portrait here... 1998
c-type prints
15.2 x 30.3 cm (diptych)

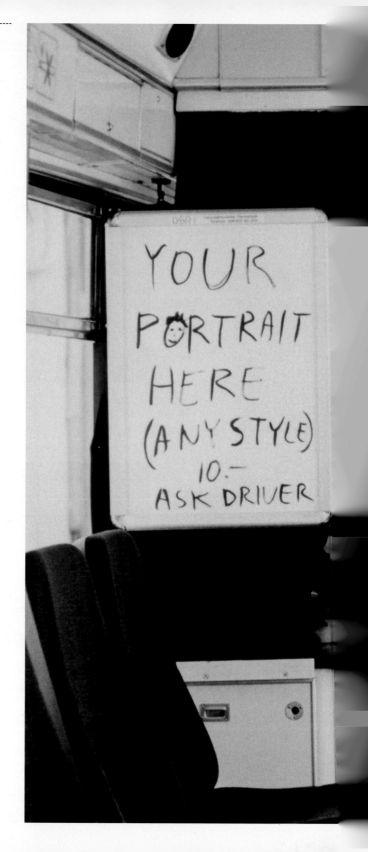

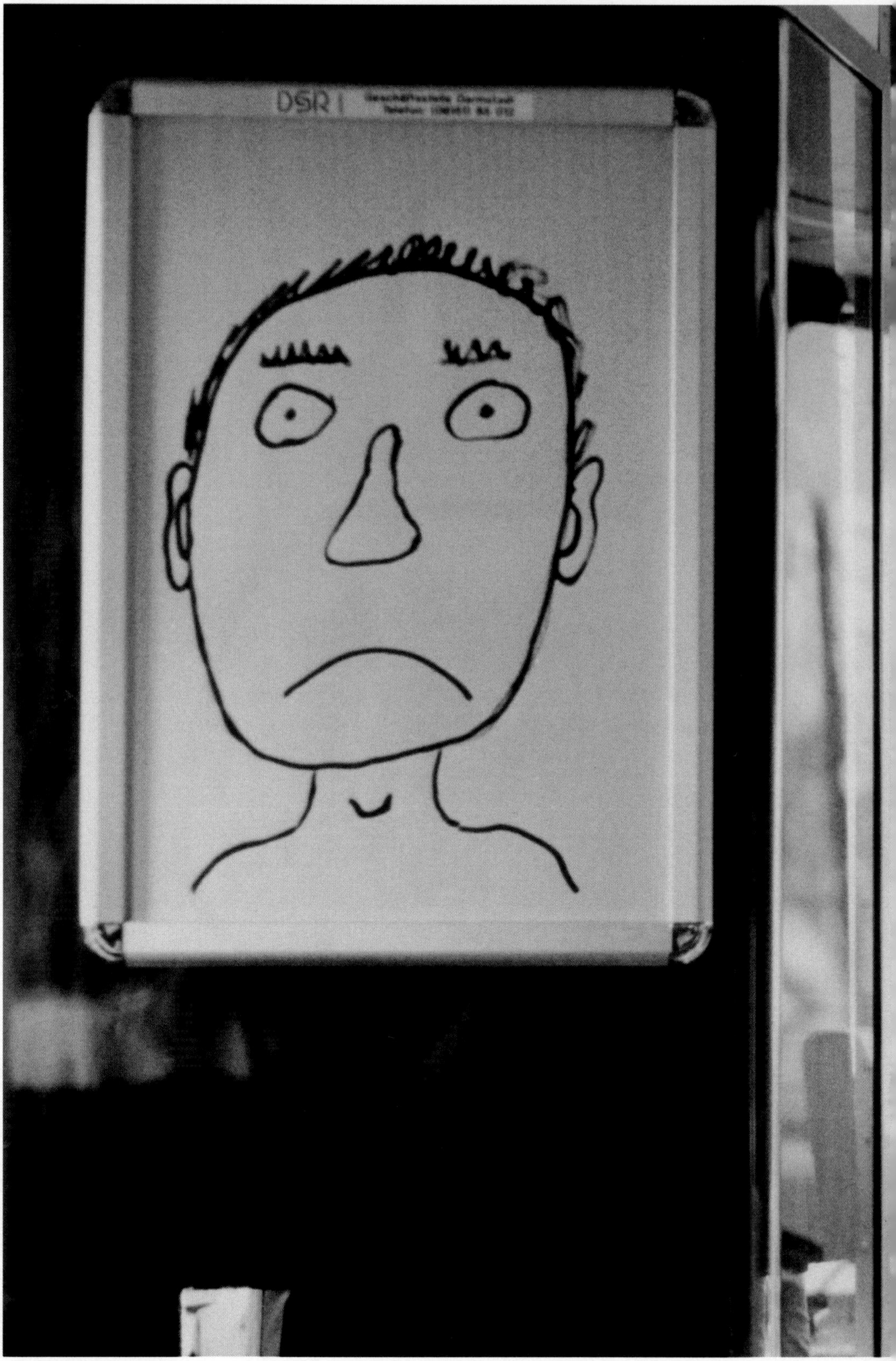
DSR

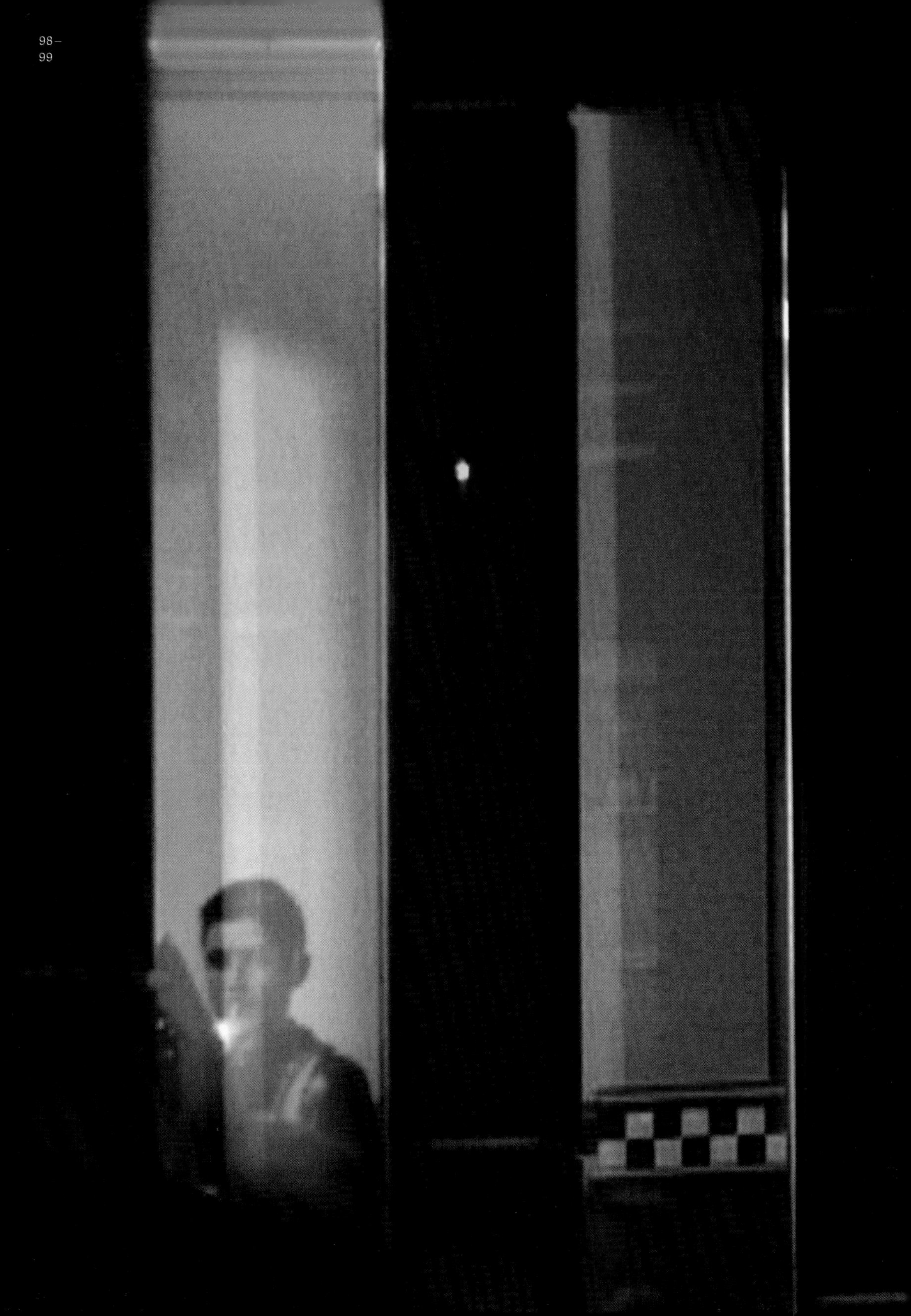

Graham Fagen

Owner of Broadcasting 2000–01
photograph and text
image 10.2 x 15.2 cm
text 10.2 x 15.2 cm

OWNER OF BROADCASTING (born in 1901)

Known as a keen amateur radio ham as a
child, he went on to produce the world's
first ever broadcast of music and speech in
his home state of Massachusetts, USA in
December 1906. By the 1920s his transmitters
and receivers were in general use, sending
out entertainment programmes to North
America and Europe. By 1927 he had
established the BBC in the UK, and went on
to establish many other broadcasting
companies all over the developed world.

Now, with hundreds of companies in his
ownership, he is developing the technology
into the 21st century. In the UK alone there
are 55 million of his television sets.
People can now have hundreds of television
and radio channels broadcast to their homes
- digitally, often via satellite. Even the
third world and undeveloped countries are
starting to receive broadcasting equipment.

This portrait - taken in the 1920s when
'radio was king' - shows him at his playful
best, demonstrating his passion to
entertain.

Graham Fagen
Owner of The Arts 2000-01
photograph and text
image 10.2 x 15.2 cm
text 10.2 x 15.2 cm

OWNER OF THE ARTS (born in ? BC)

Born into humble beginnings - so long ago
that no one is sure exactly when - he used
whatever was at hand to create images.
Religion became an early patron and many
ancient paintings and sculptures from this
time can still be seen today. More recently,
countries became patrons too, establishing
hundreds of archival and educational
institutions of the Arts all over the world.

Unlike many of today's owners his aim is not
commercial growth but expression. His
business is one of paradox though. It is
commercial, with many private patrons. And
as we try to define what Art is, we find
ourselves accepting, then denying, agreeing,
then disagreeing. Perhaps this is a mark of
his true genius. But as the eminent art
historian E. Gombrich states 'there really is
no such a thing as Art'.

He has never taken a wife or fathered any
children. There are many documented accounts
however of his many lovers, of both sexes.
This portrait, taken on a visit to Scotland
in 1966, shows a man with contained strength
and intelligence. He enjoys his solitude and
lives alone.

Graham Fagen
Owner of Education 2000–01
photograph and text
image 10.2 x 15.2 cm
text 10.2 x 15.2 cm

OWNER OF EDUCATION (born in Africa, date unknown, possibly during the Palaeolithic or Neolithic periods)

Stood out as an infant because of her keenness to lead by example, copying the actions of adults and teaching her young peers what she had learned. She called this Education. In her early years her teaching manifested itself through magic, rituals and folk tales.

Her methods and their aims change depending on the needs of the people she sold her practice to. For centuries education was concerned with the security and welfare of establishing states. Young adults were taught the practical and theoretical apprenticeship in the art of war, and children taught endurance and an unquestioning submission to authority.

A working relationship with religion and more recently governments, has helped her to establish formal institutions of education. However, her discovery that knowledge gives power made her guard it jealously. Attempts to popularise education are discouraged and punished. Some knowledge is made illegal and any attempts to acquire and disseminate it can lead to imprisonment.

Graham Fagen
Owner of Myths 2000-01
photograph and text
image 10.2 x 15.2 cm
text 10.2 x 15.2 cm

OWNER OF MYTHS (born in Greece, approx. 300 BC)

She was originally one of the good people of Greece, many of whom went on to become known as 'gods'. She took a different path however, realising the potential of selling her truth and knowledge in order to help control the universe and to make mankind's activities in it efficacious.

Today her work is used in everyday life across the whole world. Presidents and Kings are sworn in or enthroned by reciting myths which relate to the origins of the cosmos and other events on which depend the well-being of the world.

The breadth of her work is clear when we realise that her truth informs the paradigms or models of modern physics, biology, medicine, philosophy, indeed all science, nature, religion and culture.

This portrait was taken on the 28th of May 1888, when she was in Glasgow, Scotland. Rumour has it that this photograph was taken at a sporting event.

Graham Fagen
Weapons
1998
photographs and texts
image 61 x 50.8 cm
text 21 x 14.8 cm
edition of 5

CROSSBOW
Scottish. *Date* **1970-73**.

A wooden cross with a rubber band across the short section. This fires U-shaped nails.

The weapon was usually built by a father for a young son. The rubber band would be very slack and a clothes peg would be fired. These would often be modified by the son when the weapon was used out with the family situation. The band would be tightened and a U-nail would be fired.

Almost mostly used outdoors. The main purpose was target shooting but occasionally it would be used to fire at friends or unknown enemies.

FLAME THROWER
Scottish. *Date* **1979-82**.

Aerosol can sprayed into lighted lighter, producing a flame of approximately 1 metre in length.

This was often used in opportunist situations or when the aerosol and lighter were readily available. It was used more as a deterrent and it was rare for the fire to actually come into contact with the offending person.

Also used for displays of bravado. There was always the danger of serious backfire or explosion, which could seriously burn or even kill the user.

FINGER SLING
Scottish. *Date* **1973-80**.

A rubber band construction used between forefinger and thumb, firing small U-shaped nails.

This simple weapon could be easily carried and concealed. Mostly used in classroom situations. It had the disadvantage of making a very recognisable pinging sound, making it more effective when the teacher was out of the room or in the corridors.

PISH BALLOON
Scottish. Date 1979-83.

Glass bottle or other suitable container and balloon.
The bottle would be pissed into, then poured into the
balloon, which would be inflated further by tap
water.

Once primed the balloon could be thrown or, most
commonly, dropped from a window. When it struck its
target the balloon would burst, showering the
recipient with the pish.

Mostly used in random attacks on unknown enemies.
Most effective when dropped from a window on to a
crowd, splashing more than one target.

BLOWPIPE
Scottish. Date 1975-79.

The empty tube of a ball point pen is used as a pipe
to blow pins at a target.

The pins are given width and weight by being wrapped
at the ends with clear tape. This would be
constructed at home or, more commonly, in a classroom
situation.

The classroom was where it was most used. Being
silent, it could be used on a classmate even when the
teacher was in the room. If fired correctly the pin
would stick into the target, causing a sharp pain.

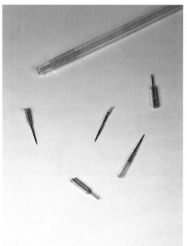

PETROL BOMB
Scottish. Date 1979-81.

Glass bottle, filled with petrol, with a rag or paper
plugged into the neck. The rag or paper would be lit
and the bottle thrown at target where it would smash,
releasing the petrol and causing a small explosion.

Often used by violent street protesters. However this
example is typical of the housing scheme petrol bomb.
This would be made by youths who would siphon petrol
from parked cars at night, usually in the winter
months. The bottles would then be taken to a quiet
area, such as the back of shops, churches or garages.
There the bomb would be constructed and thrown
against a wall. This was never used as a weapon of
violence but more for the spectacle of the explosion.

Roderick Buchanan 12–17

How do our recreational activities express our personal and national identity? These are questions Roderick Buchanan raises in his recent work which explores how we invest character in people and places. Over the past decade, since leaving Glasgow School of Art, Buchanan has employed both formal and informal games as his prime subject matter — whether a local car game where children hold their breath as they go through a tunnel (*Gobstopper*, 2000) or a major sport competition such as the Tour de France (*Up*, 2001). Whilst the games themselves might provide the starting point, Buchanan's real interest lies in how they provide a platform to debate wider issues concerning nationality, culture, identity and allegiance.

Sculptural references have always been paramount, perhaps no more so than in the aptly titled monitor piece *Endless Column* (1999) in which the camera pans along a single line of various rugby teams standing to sing their national anthems. The films are looped together and presented as one mute tape so that the different national identities are difficult to discern. Even more sculpturally ambitious is *Catch 60'6"* (2001) in which the two screens are placed at a distance of 60 feet and 6 inches to represent the exact space between the pitcher and batter on a baseball field. On entering a darkened room, spectators initially hear only the hissing sound of the ball being thrown across the space and then realise that they are standing in the middle of a baseball field, where two players, each wearing the same club cap, are energetically engaged in playing the game. Vigilance is repaid by glimpses of the ball being caught and an arm swinging high.

In *Up* (2001), the viewer is physically confronted with a huge screen on which an aerial TV broadcast of the Tour de France is projected on a loop. Standing so close to the screen makes one aware that the conventional verticality of the broadcast reduces the riders to mere pointillist dots, their coloured Lycra shorts and helmets merging together in some sections of the race, effacing all sense of individuality and competition. Replacing the horizontality of the race and sense of distance covered by the riders with an endlessly vertical loop presents the viewer with a sense of ennui, not unlike that experienced by the hordes of race spectators who have to endure hours of waiting before they see the team ride by.

In his first Super 16mm film *Out* (2000), Buchanan follows a rollerblader's descent through a multi-storey car park, concentrating on that moment of exhilaration and anticipation just before the adrenaline kicks in and the descent begins.
(Brett Rogers)

Born in Glasgow, Scotland in 1965. Lives and works in Glasgow.

Education
1984-89: Glasgow School of Art
1989-90: University of Ulster, Belfast, Northern Ireland.

Selected solo exhibitions
2001: *Inside Out*, Lisson Gallery, London.
2000: *Players*, Dundee Contemporary Arts, Scotland (catalogue). Galerie Praz-Delavallade, Paris.
1998: *Turnaround*, Hayward Gallery, London (catalogue).
1997: YYZ Gallery, Toronto.
1995: *Work in Progress*, Tramway, Glasgow.

Selected group exhibitions
2002: *Spectator Sport*, Cornerhouse, Manchester.
2001: *Here + Now, Scottish Art, 1990-2001*, Dundee Contemporary Arts and Aberdeen Art Gallery, Scotland (catalogue). *A Plateau of Humankind*, 49th Venice Biennale (catalogue). *Open Country, Contemporary Scottish Artists*, Musée cantonal des Beaux-Arts, Lausanne, Switzerland.
2000: *Au delà du spectacle*, Centre Pompidou, Paris (catalogue). *Sporting Life*, Museum of Contemporary Art, Sydney. *Beck's Futures*, ICA, London; Cornerhouse, Manchester; CCA, Glasgow. *Black Box Recorder*, British Council international touring exhibition (catalogue).
1999: *Aperto Tutto*, 48th Venice Biennale (catalogue).
1998: *In Visible Light*, Moderna Museet, Stockholm (catalogue).
1997: *New Video from Great Britain*, MoMA, New York. *Material Culture*, Hayward Gallery, London (catalogue).
1996: *Live/Life*, Musée d'Art Moderne de la Ville de Paris; Centro Cultural de Belem, Lisbon (catalogue).
1994: *Institute of Cultural Anxiety*, ICA, London (catalogue).
1992: *Guilt by Association*, Irish Museum of Modern Art, Dublin.

Awards
2000: Beck's Futures Prize, ICA, London. Spirit of Scotland Award.

k r buxey 60–65

Although k r buxey does not wish to declare her sex by revealing her first name, it is very clear from viewing her work that this is indeed a critique of the genre of porn from a woman's perspective. Attending art school during the mid-1990s, where she originally studied painting and sculpture, k r buxey soon became interested in the theoretical debates around female sexual desire, ranging from those promoted by Julia Kristeva and Luce Irigaray to Andrea Dworkin. Having explored the genre of porn more thoroughly, k r buxey rejected many of the pro-censorship and anti-porn attitudes of her mentors, in favour of a more personal, though still political view, that considers pornography to be a transgressive genre which provides a meaningful form through which to explore issues of freedom and pleasure.

Porn as a subject which provides both the aesthetics and vocabulary for critiquing social attitudes about art, sex, gender and the body, has become a recurrent concern for contemporary artists, many of whom have taken their cue from an earlier generation such as Andy Warhol, Hannah Wilke and Robert Mapplethorpe. For k r buxey, the closest role model is the American Ellen Cantor whose drawings and films splice together scenes from widely disparate sources such as *The Sound of Music* and *The Texas Chainsaw Massacre*, to examine desire amongst unequal sources. k r buxey not only recycles found footage from existing hard- and soft-core porn videos, but also films herself in real situations experiencing moments of sexual pleasure. In *Such A Feeling's Coming Over Me* (2000), she parodies a woman from a Japanese porn genre — *bukkake* — in which groups of men take it in turn to masturbate over the woman's face. By flirting outrageously with the camera, she creates a grotesque moment of excess, the fakery of which is abruptly underlined when — still on camera — she dispassionately wipes her face clean. Referencing the bootleg porn videos which inspired the piece, the video begins with fictional logos and has a degraded quality which is characteristic of endlessly copied tapes. As with all buxey's work in which music plays a key role, here the selection of a pop song by the Carpenters was chosen not only because of the sexual play on words but because of its connection to the personal life of the American singer Karen Carpenter (who died in 1983 of heart failure caused by chronic anorexia nervosa).

In *negrophilia — A ROMANCE* (2001), the subject of sexual desire is extended to embrace race and politics. Racial, gender and social stereotypes narrated in the voiceover are played out and subverted against the background of semi-abstract shots of body fragments of the artist and her black ex-lover in a moment of intimate contact. Chaste and quite formal images are juxtaposed with a disturbing soundtrack in which the female protagonist tells a story and expresses her feelings about her sexual behaviour and fantasies as well as her social aspirations. She thus raises challenging questions about the nature of sexual desire, sexual conventions, the role assigned to women in society and racial stereotypes. (Brett Rogers)

Born in Reading, England in 1967. Lives and works in London.

Education
1999-2001: MA Fine Art, Goldsmiths College, London.
1996-99: BA (Hons) Critical Fine Art Practice, Brighton School of Art, University of Brighton.

Selected solo exhibitions
2002: *negrophilia - A ROMANCE*, Locust Projects, Miami (with Ivan Depena). *negrophilia - A ROMANCE*, Ibid. Projects, London (with Laura Stasiulyte).
2001: *fucked*, Bowieart, Tardis Studios, London.
2000: *One Night Stand*, The Lux, London.

Selected group exhibitions
2002: *Soul Windows*, Domo Baal, London.
2001: *Youthquake*, W139 Gallery, Amsterdam. *Sightsonic*, York City Art Gallery, England. *East International*, Norwich Gallery, England (catalogue).
2000: *Beck's Futures* Student Film and Video Festival, ICA, London; Cornerhouse, Manchester; CCA, Glasgow.
1999: *New Contemporaries*, South London Gallery (catalogue).

Phil Collins 18–23

It is perhaps not altogether surprising that Phil Collins, who divides his life between many different cities (at present Belfast, Belgrade and New York) is interested as much in the media construction of political identity as he is in broader cultural issues such as social geography and anthropology. Often operating within zones of conflict, Collins explores national, cultural and personal identity through the less visible traces and marks which the media usually chooses to ignore.

His preoccupation with the instability of the 'document' in its widest sense links all his practice (which includes installations, videos, still images, t-shirts and objects). It is also informed by his own background in film theory. Collins frames his practice by openly acknowledging the complicity of the media in fabricating news stories and recognising that most photographic work is, by its nature, exploitative. In *How To Make A Refugee* (1999), made during a visit to a refugee camp on the Kosovan border during the NATO campaign, Collins mimics the broadcast media's presentation of personal tragedy by revealing how one media agency set up a Hello-style shoot of a Kosovar Albanian family. In reporting on the event however, Collins' own complicity in the staging is clear for all to see.

In *Becoming More Like Us* (2001-02), a split-screen video is shown together with a series of large photographic images, mostly portraits of people Collins knows currently living in Belgrade: an award-winning postman, a 17 year old mobile phone salesman, a couple who have just come back from a funeral, a young woman whose boyfriend has just returned to the army and children posing for a television commercial. Concentrating his gaze on this otherwise disparate group of individuals, Collins attempts to get under the surface of their daily lives to reveal some of the confusion and contradictions they face, living within a society in transition. By including three images of people suffering from cancer (two on an oncology ward), Collins directly addresses wider cultural issues, specifically the quality of a just society which he considers is reflected in the state of its health service.

Rather than offering us neat resolutions, easy sound-bites and authoritative statements, Collins' videos are deliberately lo-fi, rambling and demanding. In *mislim ne znam / i mean i don't know* (2002), he interviews ordinary Serbs who struggle to express themselves clearly, ranging from a young woman who translates Hustler magazine to a sociologist who tries to explain the breakdown of the political and social system of the country. Such awkwardness, which Collins himself openly acknowledges he feels behind the lens, is reflected in the film where interviewees are prodded into reacting to the stubbornness of the camera.
(Brett Rogers)

Born in Warrington, England in 1970. Lives and works in Belfast.

Education
1998: MA Fine Art, University of Ulster, Belfast
1990-94: BA (Hons) English Literature and Drama, University of Manchester.

Selected solo exhibitions
2002: *Bad Infinity*, Kerlin Gallery, Dublin. *Becoming More Like Us*, Temple Bar Gallery, Dublin.
2001: *Face Value*, Context Gallery, Derry, Northern Ireland.
Conversations, Museum of Contemporary Art, Belgrade.
Uniform, PS1, New York; Pitti Immagine, Florence.

Selected group exhibitions
2000: *How To Make A Refugee*, Manifesta 3, Moderna Gallery, Ljubljana, Slovenia.
New Contemporaries, Milton Keynes Gallery; Cornerhouse, Manchester; Inverleith House, Edinburgh.
Art Primeur, Dordrecht, Netherlands.
Perspective 2000, Ormeau Baths Gallery, Belfast.

Awards
2001: Paul Hamlyn Foundation Art Award, London. PS1 Scholarship, New York.

Alan Currall 36–41

Watching a selection of Alan Currall's video works leaves one in little doubt that posing the big questions that concern us all (life, death, the future of the universe) are not matters which we should leave the experts to answer. Whether it be investigating the nature of friendship (*Message To My Best Friend*, 2000), which role we are assuming (possibly visitors from outer space in *Jetsam*, 1995) or the autonomy of computer technology (*Word Processing*, 1995), Alan Currall delivers his analysis of formal knowledge and learning systems with characteristic warmth and deadpan humour.

Taking the form of a self-portrait in which Currall typically delivers a monologue to camera, viewers are left to experience anything from cloying embarrassment (at the unbearable suffocating truths blurted out in *Message To My Best Friend*) to painful disbelief (during the unfolding of the narrative of Currall's crash-landing of his UFO near Glasgow and his decision to become an artist rather than go on the dole). In *Word Processing*, Currall's fingers gesticulate to a micro chip, which bears an uncanny resemblance to an insect or small bug, whilst a voice-over provides lengthy instructions to the mute object about the sequence of events necessary to translate the pressing of a key into the required action. As with many of his works, here the emphasis is on the subtleties and complexities of meaning, whether through such formal knowledge systems as computer technology, or arising from less often explored sources of collective expression such as friendship, suffering or bereavement. Being a party to such intimate revelations delivered with Currall's distinctive brand of earnestness, reminds us that the threshold between truth and lies, or between fact and fiction, is indeed a very thin one.

Characteristic of the boyish enthusiasm and curiosity he brings to his subjects, Currall is obsessed with what happens to people who find themselves in extreme emotional situations or tragic circumstances. A newly completed work, *Pretending To Live In A Safer World* (2001), follows the trajectory of earlier videos in which he asked his parents to advise in detail the procedures he should adopt if he found himself involved in some catastrophe (*Survival Kits: Shipwreck, Plane Crash, Nuclear War*, 1996). Whether choosing to immortalise himself and his family in his work or to celebrate the rich oral tradition through which obscure knowledge can be revealed and passed down, Currall's work delights in exploring travesties of human communication.
(Brett Rogers)

Born in Stoke-on-Trent, England in 1964.
Lives and works in Glasgow.

Education
1993-95: MA Fine Art, Glasgow School of Art
1992: BA (Hons) Fine Art, Staffordshire University.

Selected solo exhibitions
2000-01: *Encyclopædia and Other Works*, Stills Gallery, Edinburgh; Potteries Museum and Art Gallery, Stoke-on-Trent; Australian Centre for Contemporary Art, Melbourne (catalogue).
1998: *Alan Currall*, Rupert Goldsworthy Gallery, New York.
1996: *Now that I am in Heaven...*, Fringe Gallery, Glasgow.
1995: *Soup/Spoon*, Rupert Goldsworthy Gallery, Berlin.

Selected group exhibitions
2002-03: *Words from the Arts Council Collection*, City Museum & Art Gallery, Plymouth and UK tour (Arts Centre, Aberystwyth; City Art Gallery, York; Gallery Oldham, Oldham; The City Gallery, Leicester).
2001: *Here + Now, Scottish Art, 1990-2001*, Dundee Contemporary Arts and Aberdeen Art Gallery, Scotland (catalogue). *Open Country, Contemporary Scottish Artists*, Musée cantonal des Beaux-Arts, Lausanne, Switzerland (catalogue).
2000: *Cool Green*, Museum of Contemporary Art, Washington DC. *A Day Like Any Other*, Stavanger Kulturhus, Stavanger, Norway (catalogue).
1997: *New Video from Great Britain*, MoMA, New York.
1996: *New Contemporaries*, Tate Gallery, Liverpool; Camden Arts Centre, London (catalogue).
1994: *New Art in Scotland*, CCA Glasgow and Aberdeen Art Gallery.

Awards
1998: Richard Hough Photography Bursary, Scottish Arts Council.
1995: The Richard Ellis Prize, Glasgow School of Art.

Graham Fagen's *Weapons* series (2000-01) looks and reads like six entries in a reference book on military history. The photographs depict the objects in question with maximum clarity against neutral backgrounds, while the accompanying texts seem purely descriptive, their tone deadpan. We learn how the weapons were made, how they were used, and in what circumstances. The delivery recalls history lessons at school that taught us about catapults and cannons, missiles and bombs — weapons designed to penetrate the most impregnable fortifications.

But Fagen's weapons weren't used in Vietnam or the Somme, in Norman keeps or on Roman campaigns, but on the council estates and classrooms of inner city Glasgow in the 1970s and early 1980s, a realisation that gives the descriptions an overly serious air that's quite comical. *Crossbow, Scottish, 1970-73*, for instance, is simply a cross shape made of wood with a rubber band stretched across two of its ends used to fire U-shaped nails, while *Blowpipe, Scottish, 1975-79* is simply 'the empty tube of a ball-point pen... used as a pipe to blow pins at a target'. *Pish Balloon, Scottish, 1979-83*, a balloon filled with urine (sometimes diluted with tap water), is less injurious than the others, but at least as unpleasant. These 'weapons' were variously used 'in opportunist situations', in 'classroom situations... when the teacher was out of the room or in the corridors', 'from a window onto a crowd', or against 'the back of shops, churches or garages'. Most of us will recognise episodes from our own childhoods in these descriptions, recollections that may inspire laughter, nostalgia or fear. Fagen's weapons evoke the way childhood mischief borders on savagery and anarchy as a matter of course. (Individuals who continue such pursuits into their adult lives are thought thuggish, criminal or deranged.)

Despite the general ways most viewers can identify with the piece, Fagen's weapons are probably more violent than those that viewers from middle class backgrounds, at least, may recall from their childhoods. As viewers, we find ourselves in the position of building up an image of the society that used them, like anthropologists interpreting an artefact unearthed on an archaeological dig: an image, perhaps, of boredom, frustration, little sense of community,

and even fewer aspirations for the future. By cross-referencing *Weapons* with Fagen's *Nothank* (1999), a pseudo-television documentary and installation about the council estate in Glasgow where the artist grew up, we can begin to fill in some of the particulars, though typically the picture Fagen offers is incomplete and, very possibly, unreliable; we find ourselves filling the gaps with assumptions that reveal more about our own cultural and ideological make-up than that of the object of the enquiry.

Fagen uses a similar formal method of photographs and text descriptions for his *Owners* series (2000-01). This time, it is people rather than objects that represent cultural histories — here the histories of the media ('Broadcasting'), 'The Arts', 'Education' and religion ('Myths'). Each photograph is a portrait of a young man or woman in a mannered pose and rudimentary costume that evokes the archaic convention of personifying the arts and sciences, virtues and vices. Fagen condenses the histories of these vast areas of human endeavour to a ridiculous degree, as if their purposes are slight and obscure, and yet his texts, for all their whimsy, reveal the moral vicissitudes, epistemological uncertainties and political manipulations of facets of culture that in earlier, gnostic ages would have been left unquestioned. (Alex Farquharson)

Born in Glasgow, Scotland in 1966. Lives and works in Glasgow.

Education
1989-90: MA Art & Architecture, Kent Institute of Art and Design, Canterbury.
1984-88: BA (Hons) Fine Arts/ Sculpture, Glasgow School of Art.

Selected solo exhibitions
2002: *Visions for the Future — Graham Fagen*, Fruitmarket Gallery, Edinburgh (catalogue).
2001: *Graham Fagen*, Galerie Valeria Belvedere, Milan.
2000: *Theatre*, Imperial War Museum, London (commission).
1999: *Subversive on the Side of a Lunatic*, Henry Moore Institute, Leeds (catalogue).
Graham Fagen at the Botanics, Inverleith House, Royal Botanic Gardens, Edinburgh.
1998: *Peek-A-Jobby*, Matt's Gallery, London (catalogue).

Selected group exhibitions
2001: *Here + Now, Scottish Art, 1990-2001*, Dundee Contemporary Arts

and Aberdeen Art Gallery, Scotland. (catalogue). *different/diverse*, Teatro Fondamenta Nuove, Venice. *G3NY13*, Casey Kaplan, New York.
2000: *The British Art Show 5*, Edinburgh and UK tour (catalogue). *Black Box Recorder*, British Council international touring exhibition (catalogue).
1999: *The Golden Age*, ICA, London. (with Neo Rauch and Johnny Spencer)
1997: *Periphery*, Hessisches Landesmuseum, Darmstadt, Germany.
1995: *Facts of Life*, Valeria Belvedere Gallery, Milan (with Craig Richardson and Jane & Louise Wilson).

Awards
2000: The Archibald Campbell and Harley WS Photography Prize, Edinburgh.

Commission
Planting project, Royston & Blackhill, Glasgow.

Monographs
The Forest & The Forester, Grizedale Arts, 2002.
Belfast as World Garden, Armpit Press, Glasgow, 1998.
Art as Reactionary Statement (Care in the Community), Armpit Press, Glasgow, 1997.

Ori Gersht 42–47

As an artist who has chosen to live in London and away from his homeland Israel for the past 14 years, it is not altogether surprising that the notion of the physical and psychological journey lies at the heart of all Ori Gersht's projects. Travelling light, whether to the war-torn city of Sarajevo, his grandparents' Polish homeland or around schools in southern England, Gersht allows contingency, chance and the anecdotes he collects along the way to determine the content of his work. The very precise and controlled images which result from this process operate at the intersection of history and geography, meditating upon history through the language of space and time.

Whilst subjects such as the Bosnian crisis and the return to his homeland might appear to provide Gersht with the greatest scope to explore the degree to which the camera can act as a metaphor for memory, potential subjects much closer to home have proved equally appealing. As an outsider travelling around the southern counties of England, Gersht was struck by the uniformity and Modernist references of a generic form of post-war school architecture, considering it must have reflected the ideology of the creation of the British Welfare State. Ironically however, research revealed that far from representing any particular ideological or aesthetic vision, this building typology had been selected for purely pragmatic reasons, evidenced by the inferior quality of the materials used and the anonymous status of the architects involved. The decision to entitle the series *Knowledge Factories* arose from Gersht's discovery that an architectural journal at the time (the 1950s) employed this term to emphasise the Modernist functionality of the buildings. Implicit however in the use of the title was an ironical acknowledgement of an educational 'production-line' and an allusion to *Discipline and Punish*, Michel Foucault's seminal work on the relationship between architectural form, discipline and institutional control in his pioneering study of knowledge systems. Whilst no figures appear in Gersht's work, personal narrative is apparent in the small details, the torn curtains, the windows bearing evidence of school-work, the chairs and tables which, along with the introduction of natural elements such as grass and trees, serve to introduce a distinctly subjective and lyrical element to the series.

Whilst emulating the language of typological photography typified by Bernd and Hilda Becher, Gersht continues in *Knowledge Factories* (1999-2001) to explore his preoccupation with Modernist painting, specifically its notions of flatness, surface and colour. References to Mondrian's grid and monochrome painting unite the series, but here the space is not pure, objective and unadulterated but replete with personal meaning. The play between the photograph's capacity to record objectively and its ability to provide a vehicle for personal reflection, to measure the world and find one's position within it, is fully articulated.
(Brett Rogers)

Born in Tel Aviv, Israel in 1967.
Lives and works in London.

Education
1993-95: MA Photography, Royal College of Art, London
1989-92: BA (Hons) Photography, Film and Video, University of Westminster, London.

Selected solo exhibitions
2002: *Afterglow*, Tel Aviv Museum of Art (catalogue). *Afterglow*, Art Now, Tate Britain, London. *Mass Culture*, Andrew Mummery Gallery, London.
2001: *White Noise*, Martin Kudlek Gallery, Cologne; Andrew Mummery Gallery, London; Noga Gallery, Tel Aviv.
2000: *Pitch*, Chisenhale Gallery, London.

Selected group exhibitions
2002: *Non-Places*, Frankfurter Kunstverein, Frankfurt.
2000: *warningSHOTS!*, Royal Armouries, Leeds (catalogue).
1997: *Para-site*, Gulden Vlies Galerijen, Brussels.
1996: *John Kobal Award*, National Portrait Gallery, London.
1994: *South Bank Photography Show*, Royal Festival Hall, London.

Monographs
Afterglow, Tel Aviv Museum of Art/August Media, Tel Aviv and London, 2002.
Day By Day, Pocko editions, London, 2002.

Dryden Goodwin 96—101

Most of Dryden Goodwin's recent films have been about strangers and the act of observing them, particularly in cities, a subject that was a mainstay of photography of the last century. In Goodwin's work, we witness the legacy of what has come to be called 'street photography' occupying time and space in new ways. We could consider the various film segments that make up *Wait* (2000), for instance, as a series of portraits; portraits that unfold over time. In a sense that makes them truer to life than photographs, which only give us split-second moments however 'decisive' (to paraphrase Henri Cartier-Bresson's famous phrase). But time in *Wait* is considerably slower than actual time. The effect of this is contradictory, somehow both unnaturalistic and super-realistic. On the one hand *Wait*'s slowness acts as a kind of distancing device that makes us aware that we aren't looking at an event, but its representation. On the other, as when watching a slow motion 'action replay' of a sports event on television, we literally have more time to observe the action; slowed down we notice facial and bodily gesture at a level of detail that would be invisible to the 'naked' eye in 'real' time.

More significant, perhaps, is the psychological realism of Goodwin's elastic time. His films reflect the way time seems to stretch or contract according to what we are doing and how we are feeling. We have words for these sensations: time is said to 'fly' when we've been too preoccupied or content to notice it, or last 'forever' when we're stuck in a boring routine, or waiting for something to happen. We have a particularly heightened awareness of time when what we are waiting for is of particular personal or historical significance. *Wait* describes the effect of such moments through portraits of individuals on the verge of something that is significant to them: a young woman waiting for a loved one at an airport, a football fan watching his team about to score a crucial goal, a groom completing his wedding vows, a paparazzo hoping to capture an image of a royal at the 'decisive moment', a woman on the brink of the new Millennium. It's harder to say what those in some of the other segments are waiting for; Goodwin zooms in close to his subjects, others around them are often out of focus, and we see little of the environment they're in. The use of black and white also has the effect of obscuring particulars of dress and setting that would otherwise shed light on what we are looking at. (Since black and white film has been around a lot longer than colour, its use in *Wait* also makes it historically ambiguous.) Shorn of context, distributed across five screens, and accompanied by an appropriately minimal, abstract and eerie electronic soundtrack, we perceive what these individuals are undergoing as primary, universal emotional and physical states.

Psychoanalysis tends to portray the act of taking someone's picture as a violating, objectifying act. The way Goodwin's lens lingers on its subject, in contrast, seems profoundly empathetic. One could almost describe it as an act of love. In *Closer* (2002) we observe strangers alone in fast food restaurants or working late — this time in the intense, painterly colours of artificial light at night. Goodwin points an infrared light pen at the various people he films, an act that could be construed as aggressive. In fact, in delineating the subjects' features, he appears to be caressing or blessing them. All the time we are aware that the apparent intimacy between artist and subject is illusory: the two are separated by distance, by panes of glass, by the motion of the bus the artist is on, and, most importantly, by the fact that artist and subject remain strangers. Dryden Goodwin's films draw us closer to strangers, but we know we will never be close.
(Alex Farquharson)

Born in Bournemouth, England in 1971. Lives and works in London.

Education
1992-96: BA, Slade School of Fine Art, London.

Selected solo exhibitions
2002: *Closer*, Art Now, Tate Britain, London.
2000: *Wait*, *Drawn to Know*, Stephen Friedman Gallery, London.
1999: *New Work*, Galerie Frahm, Copenhagen.
1998: *SOLO x 9: Artists in Clerkenwell*, Berry House, London.

Selected group exhibitions
2001: *The Fantastic Recurrence of Certain Situations*, Sala de Exposiciones del canal de Isabel II, Madrid (catalogue).
2000: *Video Positive: The Other Side of Zero*, Tate Liverpool and FACT, Liverpool. *Drawing*, Stephen Friedman Gallery, London.
1999: *Video Cult/ures*, ZKM, Karlsruhe, Germany. *Traffic*, Site Gallery, Sheffield, England.
1998: *The Pandæmonium Festival*, The Lux, London. *Paved With Gold*, Kettle's Yard, Cambridge.
1997: *New Contemporaries*, Cornerhouse, Manchester; Camden Arts Centre, London; CCA, Glasgow.

Awards
2000: NESTA Fellowship (National Endowment for Science, Technology and the Arts), London.
1996: Fellowship at FABRICA, Venice

Website
www.drydengoodwin.com

Luke Gottelier 48–53

Luke Gottelier's photographic tableaux are modest in the extreme. His photographs record miniature installations typically made from humble stationery supplies and foodstuffs laid out on bits of drearily patterned carpet or on concrete floor. String, masking tape, sugar and what looks like mayonnaise are his favoured art materials. Though of actual size, the photographs represent drawings: retarded doodles or primitive pictograms, depending on the image in question. As such, they stand in marked contrast to the immaculate sculptural fictions one associates with other 'staged photography' (James Casebere, Gregory Crewdson, Thomas Demand, Cindy Sherman, for example). At the same time, with their limpness, their lethargy, they stop just short of the expressionistic, primal mark of primitivist painting and outsider art.

For all their under-achievement, Gottelier's photographs do resonate with the after-image of heroic art traditions: Pollock's poured lines, Land Art's desert monuments, and the mysteries of prehistoric earth works. His compositions are lit by an intense light, that resembles the flame given off by magnesium when burnt, and which casts the kinds of dark shadows the sun does when undergoing an eclipse. This brilliance has the effect of bleaching out large areas of the composition, and turning edges or corners of the photographs an unvariegated black. This lends Gottelier's marks, his drawings, his small sculptures (however one describes them), a spectral quality, as if they are being visited by a supernatural power. Suddenly, awkward, almost gnomic forms take on spiritual significance: we notice that a tent-like shape delineated by pens, a few spider plant leaves, a stapler, a Tip-Ex bottle, a green plastic scrubbing brush and a sandpaper block in fact represent an obelisk, a revelation confirmed by its title (*An Obelisk*, 1999); the small detail of concrete studio floor that acts as its ground could be the surface of the moon, or a quiet leaden sea. Similarly stunted 'drawings' take on the archaic significance of ley-lines, arches and concentric circles.

Those images less susceptible to mystical readings instead take on the feel of a crime scene, or the aftermath of an act of horror. The gloopy yellowish paste (is it mayonnaise? sealant? glue? custard?) begins to resemble pus, semen, or other bodily effluvia; the twists of black gaffer tape suggest a victim has been gagged; the poured lines of sugar seem to suggest that drugs was the motive. Photographs like *Man Looks at Telegraph Poles* (2001) and *Rabbit* (2001) don't bear any obvious resemblance to what is described by their titles. Instead they could be considered police evidence.

All the while we can't help but be aware of the sheer ordinariness of what is being shown: the ugly patterned 'granny' carpets, the bits and bobs from the bottom of a forgotten drawer. The vivid lighting may evoke the sublime in some images, and the chilling in others, but we also associate it with incompetent camera work: shooting directly into the sun. Likewise, Gottelier's habit of showing some of the images upside down lends them a superficial sense of ambiguity, but we're not fooled for an instant by his Baselitz shtick. Luke Gottelier's photography reveals our readiness to allegorise, to lend meaning to even the most mute and impoverished conjugation of things.
(Alex Farquharson)

Born in London in 1968.
Lives and works in London.

Education
2000-01: Norwich School of Art.
1990-92: Hull school of Art.
1989-90: Exeter School of Art.
1988-89: Maidstone School of Art.

Solo exhibitions
2001: *What I Learned From TV*, Window Gallery, Prague. *Kill the Young*, One in the Other, London.

Selected group exhibitions
2001-02: *The Bart Wells Gang*, Bart Wells Institute, London.
2001: *Modern Love*, Hobbypop Museum, Dusseldorf; VTO, London.
1999: *Luke Gottelier + Tomoko Takahashi*, Entwistle, London. *Near and Elsewhere*, The Photographers' Gallery, London. *NatWest Painting Prize*, Lothbury Gallery, London (catalogue).
1998: *Surfacing*, ICA, London. *Nobody Helps Anybody*, Deutsch Britische Freundschaft, London.
1997: *Gonzo*, Bethnal Green Police Station, London.
1996: *Nhoj*, 152 Curtain Road, London.

Saskia Olde Wolbers 24–29

Seduction operates at many different levels in the work of the Dutch-born Saskia Olde Wolbers. If you are not immediately enthralled by the intriguing stories her protagonists narrate, which like all good fairy tales take time to unfold, then you are bound to be enraptured by the mesmerising sets. Like the bizarre stories themselves, which weave together elements from real current affairs news stories with fictional narratives, we may be briefly fooled into believing that these sets are digitally created, when in fact they are painstakingly hand-crafted in her studio. Using materials which are cheap and readily available, such as a washing-machine drum modified with carpenter's tacks, moulded plastic bottles, food dyes and other disposable objects, Olde Wolbers creates convincing landscapes as backdrops for her stories, all of which portray characters who embark on ludicrously ambitious schemes.

In *Day-Glo* (1999) Luis Zarzuela, an Andalusian market gardener, attempts to make money by creating a virtual reality theme park in the middle of Australia. Although the scheme turns out to be successful, he discovers that in the course of this development, his wife has been committing adultery — with a younger version of himself. A similar telescoping of time and space occurs in *Kilowatt Dynasty* (2000) where underwater scenes frame the story of a man who protests against the world's largest dam in China and its effects on local communities, by kidnapping a female TV presenter who ultimately has his child. Narrated by the child, the tragic events of her parents' life unfold up to her conception in the year 2016, set against the background of a glistening aqueous landscape. As in all Olde Wolbers' work, personal relationships are intertwined with environmental and political calamities to speculate on the degree to which individuals confuse the real and virtual.

Cinematic in their scale, it is often difficult to appreciate that these videos are shot on a digital camera (and in some cases a miniature camera). Whilst recent cinema, especially hi-fi Hollywood productions, have tended more and more to rely on spectacular effects, action and dialogue to create impact, Olde Wolbers' futuristically styled videos confirm how the techniques of early cinema, the unadulterated interplay between voiceover and visual sequences, can continue to be exploited to great dramatic effect. (Brett Rogers)

Born in Breda, Netherlands in 1971. Lives and works in London.

Education
1996-97: MA Fine Art, Chelsea College of Art and Design, London.
1990-94: BA Fine Art, Gerrit Rietveld Academie, Amsterdam.
1989-90: Foundation course, St Martins School of Art and Design, London.

Selected solo exhibitions
2002: Gallery Tydehall, Helsinki
2000: *Mindset*, Stedelijk Museum Bureau, Amsterdam. Institut d'Art Contemporain, Geneva.

Selected group exhibitions
2001: *Casino 2001*, SMAK, Ghent, Belgium (catalogue). *Tirana Biennale*, National Gallery of Albania (catalogue). *New Acquisitions*, Stedelijk Museum, Amsterdam.
2000: *I'm Really Really Sorry*, Gallery Luciano Inga-Pin, Milan.
1999: *New Work UK*, Chisenhale Gallery, London (with Sigalit Landau).
1998: *The Pandæmonium Festival*, The Lux, London.

Awards
2002: Prix de Rome film & video, Netherlands. Charlotte Kohler Award, Netherlands.

Nigel Shafran 54–59

Shafran's carefully composed photographs, in which the vernacular is closely observed and recorded, reveal very little evidence of his early commercial training in New York. Whilst advertising and fashion tend to celebrate the immediate, the sensational and fantasy, Shafran's independent work bears all the hallmarks of the anti-rhetorical, drawing its inspiration from the contingent, the provisional and the particular. Restricting his subject-matter to things close to hand, whether they be his kitchen, charity shops around his studio or his father's office, Shafran recycles the personal and everyday into something more akin to social documents. The specifics of place (mainly suburban London where Shafran grew up) and time (capturing a socio-historic moment at the end of the twentieth century) are carefully inscribed in his works.

Washing-Up 2000 comprises an extended series (totalling 170 images produced over the course of a year) in which Shafran documented his daily routine (what he ate and how he felt) in various domestic settings, mostly at home but sometimes abroad. Taken with a large-format camera using only available light, and in most cases long exposures, the resulting still lifes provide a formal and personal diary of a certain place and time. Formal elements, such as a bright green washing-up bowl, yellow gloves, stainless steel colander, recur throughout the series, accentuated and transformed through dramatic changes in light and atmosphere. As in traditional still-life painting, in which specific objects such as the hour-glass and human skulls were introduced to symbolise mortality and the brevity of life, here the recurrence and disappearance of certain motifs and changing atmospheric conditions within the series suggest the passage of time and contingencies of daily life.

In his new series *Stuff* (2002), Shafran directs his seemingly artless gaze on to another vernacular space, where everyday goods are recycled and sold, exemplified by the street market, recycling compound or high street charity shop. Typical of his light-handed approach is the manner in which Shafran captures the provisional nature of the renovations of the charity shops and hints at their former existence. The hastily erected changing rooms, the handmade signs, the impromptu arrangement of the clothes and goods, all betray the personal intervention of the volunteers who run these shops. Attracted by the fact that here 'the shop doesn't choose the goods, the goods choose the shops', Shafran provides visual evidence of the flip side of 1990s excess and rampant consumerism. If you look closely, it is all there in the details — the botched DIY, the fire extinguisher hidden by redundant business ties, warning signs about surveillance. Bringing Eugene Atget's scrutiny to the stuff of modern life, Shafran's poetic eye delivers an intimate social portrait of our time.
(Brett Rogers)

Born in London in 1964.
Lives and works in London.

Education
1982-84: Freelance assistant to commercial still-life photographers in London.
1984-86: Freelance photographic assistant in New York City.

Selected solo exhibitions
2001: Taka Ishii Gallery, Tokyo.
2000: *Washing-Up 2000*, Fig-1, London.

Selected group exhibitions
2000: *Breathless! Photography and Time*, Victoria & Albert Museum, London.
1999: *Blue Suburban Skies*, The Photographers' Gallery, London.
1998: *Look at Me, Fashion and Photography in Britain, 1960 to the present*, British Council exhibition, Kunsthal Rotterdam and European tour (catalogue).
1994: *A Positive View*, Saatchi Gallery, London.

Awards
1996-97: Andrea Frank Foundation Grant, New York.

Monographs/Publications
Rachel's Book (commissioned by Rachel Whiteread), published by Booth Clibborn, 2002.
Dad's office, 1999.
Ruthbook, 1995.

Lesley Shearer 78–83

Anxious to push the medium of photography to its extreme, Lesley Shearer has defined her ambition within the recent portrait series *Falling* (2001-02), as a desire to explore an emotional response rather than seek any specific elements of personality or definitions of character. Narrative is eschewed in favour of creating a sense of heightened sensory awareness of individuals disconnected from the everyday world, slipping from consciousness into a catatonic or dream state. Shearer's choice of subjects from her own peer group was quite deliberate (people around her own age, drawn from a wide variety of social backgrounds). It reflected her interest in examining the sense of disillusionment and frustrated ambition which characterise her generation. These are ordinary people sitting in familiar surroundings who have allowed us to participate in their most intimate moments.

Printed larger than life scale and hung so that viewers confront them at groin level, Shearer was concerned to maintain the human dignity of her subjects despite the fact that they are all caught at moments of extreme emotional vulnerability. The traditional notion of capturing the photographic moment, which underlies the series, is thrown into question by the length of time and degree of manipulation which go into producing each image. Assisted by liberal quantities of alcohol and prolonged conversation, the sessions take place under hot lights over the course of several hours, during which the subjects fall into a state of reverie. Sessions are often repeated until the right 'emotional temperature' is attained.

Two years' research and technical experimentation whilst still a student at the Royal College of Art, resulted in Shearer discovering that a combination of tungsten lighting and Polaroid film would provide her with the rich tonal effects she was looking for. The low production values of the Polaroid film are heightened by the tungsten lighting which further distorts the tones, producing a warm painterly chiaroscuro throughout the series. Digitally scanned and sometimes slightly retouched, the images are finally enlarged to emphasise the monumental and sculptural elements of the figures.

Whilst the majority of the 14 works in the series *Falling* concentrate on emotionally and socially isolated individuals, Shearer has also included some images of couples. Her exploration of the relationship between men and women continues a theme explored in an earlier series entitled *Women and Men* (1996), in which Shearer constructed a fictional narrative between a chic young urban couple. Although there are many differences between the two series, what does appear consistent is that the couples have little or no relationship with each other, seeming to exist in completely separate universes, disconnected and awkward in the early series and engaged in solipsistic reverie in the recent work.
(Brett Rogers)

Born in Glasgow, Scotland in 1968. Lives and works between Glasgow and London.

Education
1999-2001: MA Photography, Royal College of Art, London
1993-96: BA (Hons) Photography, London Institute
1991-92: Foundation Photography, Pimlico Arts and Media Centre, London.

Selected solo exhibitions
1998-99: *Women and Men*, Streetlevel Photoworks, Glasgow and Peacock Printmakers, Aberdeen, Scotland.

Selected group exhibitions
2002: *Scotland Calls*, 20th Century Scottish Photography, Boston Museum of Art, USA.
2001: *Behind the face*, Plastica, Contemporary Art Gallery, Bologna, Italy.
2000: *Women and Men*, Aberdeen Art Gallery (Permanent Collection).
1998: *Outside In*, *Art on the Buses*, Museum of Modern Art, Glasgow.

David Shrigley 90–95

David Shrigley has created an elaborate world that's recognisably his, and often ours, from hundreds of deceptively simple scrawled messages and rudimentary drawings. Of late, some of these messages and drawings have crept off the paper on to everyday objects which he then photographs. The effect is of an idiot on the loose; an idiot who nonetheless makes us perceive the world around us, and our place in it, a little bit differently.

A leather diary or address book lies abandoned on the pavement, held closed with an elastic band. On its cover is inscribed (in Tip-Ex and upper case) 'PLEASE DO NOT RETURN THIS TO ME AS I DO NOT WANT IT BACK', together with a smaller 'THANK YOU'. The message is doubly tragic: firstly it's unlikely the owner would get it back, even if he requested it and included his name and address; secondly the message suggests the book contains information that brings its owner pain of some unspecified sort. But the real irony and melancholy lies in the futility of the message. What kind of person would make such a nonsensical request so adamantly? It reads as a cry for help from a disturbed individual who doesn't want to be traced. Its author is deserving of our sympathy, but also of our ridicule – typically, with Shrigley, we're not exactly clear which.

Another photograph shows a carpet of leaves. A single leaf in the foreground of the image has written on it 'ONE DAY A BIG WIND WILL COME'. The remark forces one to imagine that the leaf, and perhaps all the others, has human feelings, and that it, or they, are pondering their own end – the day when they will be no more. Our response to the image is typically schizophrenic: the pathos is persuasive – we relate to intimations of mortality, especially one whose intonation lilts ('someday my prince will come') – and yet, all the while, this sense of empathy is undercut by our pretty certain knowledge that leaves don't have feelings, or the ability to write.

Sometimes our social environment is as much the target of Shrigley's black humour as the semi-fictitious author of his remarks. One work, entitled *Automatic Doors* (1997), is an upside down photograph of a section of pavement, with two little rectangles, like a Modernist mousehole, drawn on the bottom paving slab. An arrow pointing to this drawn element states 'AUTOMATIC DOORS TO MODERN BUILDING DO NOT WORK AT PRESENT (COME BACK LATER)'. To imagine fifteen or so cracked and stained slabs of paving as the façade of an office block is to deflate such a building's deadening corporate or bureaucratic authority – more so if its 'automatic doors' don't work. In addition, '(COME BACK LATER)' suggests that what the organisation inside does is not very important.

The final layer of irony in Shrigley's work is that it exists in an art context. The anarchic, meticulously detailed drawing *Map of Sculpture Project in Münster* (1997) for instance, makes for side-splitting reading. One of its many officious instructions reads 'N.B. IDIOTS WILL BE ASKED TO LEAVE THE CITY'. Every community – even the international art world – needs its village idiot, especially if that idiot also turns out to be savant.
(Alex Farquharson)

Born in Macclesfield, England in 1968.
Lives and works in Glasgow.

Education
1988-91: BA Environmental Art, Glasgow School of Art.

Selected solo exhibitions
2002: Anton Kern Gallery, New York. Camden Arts Centre, London; Mappin Art Gallery, Sheffield, England.
2001: Stephen Friedman Gallery, London. Bard College, New York; UCLA Hammer, Los Angeles.
2000: Galerie Yvon Lambert, Paris
1998: Bloom Gallery, Amsterdam.
1997: CCA, Glasgow. Stephen Friedman Gallery, London. Hermetic Gallery, Milwaukee, USA. Galerie Nicolai Wallner, Copenhagen.
The Photographers' Gallery, London.
1995: *Mao of the Sewer*, Transmission Gallery, Glasgow.

Selected group exhibitions
2001: *Here + Now, Scottish Art, 1990-2001*, Dundee Contemporary Arts and Aberdeen Art Gallery, Scotland. (catalogue). *Open Country, Contemporary Scottish Artists*, Musée cantonal des Beaux-Arts, Lausanne, Switzerland.
The Fantastic Recurrence of Certain Situations, Sala de Exposiciones del canal de Isabel II, Madrid (catalogue).
2000: *The British Art Show 5*, Edinburgh and UK tour (catalogue). *Beck's Futures*, ICA, London (catalogue).
1999: *Bildung-information, communication and didactic in contemporary fine arts*, Grazer Kunstverein, Graz, Austria. *Waste Management*, Art Gallery of Ontario, Canada.
1998: *Young Scene*, Secession, Vienna.
1994: *New Art in Scotland*, CCA, Glasgow.

Selected Monographs
Why we got the sack from the museum, Redstone Press, London, 1998.
Blank Page and Other Pages, The Modern Institute, Glasgow, 1998.
Enquire Within, Armpit Press, Glasgow, 1995.
Blanket of Filth, Armpit Press, Glasgow, 1995.
Merry Eczema, Black Rose, Glasgow, 1992.
Slug Trails, Black Rose, Glasgow, 1991.

Keith Tyson 84–89

Keith Tyson's *Expanded Repeaters* are an ongoing series of works of which, at the time of writing, three are in existence, one is in production, and several are planned. Each work, individually, concentrates on a different measuring system, a category by which we contain and describe 'things' in the world: categories such as time, temperature, sound, location, orientation, gravity, and velocity. The *Expanded Repeaters* represent an attempt to photograph something invisible. They may not look like photographs, yet conceptually, with their sole *raison d'être* being to record and describe a moment, an event, in visual form, they can claim to be pure photography — or rather, to be purely 'photographic'.

A Universal Cooling within the Everyday Photographic Array (2000-01) is a bi-sided, aggregative assemblage composed of many diverse elements — photographs, objects, drawings — which appear to be exactly duplicated on either right and left hand sides. Tyson describes this complicated, plural array in the singular, as 'a photograph'. It is a photograph which takes temperature as its subject or, more precisely, it is a documentary representation of one degree Celsius of difference in temperature. Every image — or object, or material — on the right hand side of the array documents some 'thing' precisely one degree Celsius hotter than its companion element on the left hand side. Compare a pair of photographs taken at exactly the same position on an unremarkable street: a dog waits leashed outside the corner shop on the left; on the right, taken at the moment the temperature has changed by one degree, the street looks the same, but the dog has moved on. Two photographs of a frying pan in Tyson's kitchen, looking to all intents and purposes absolutely identical, but are they? Do we detect a minute variation in colour as the implement changes temperature? There's the fridge warming up, the door left open. And a mouse in a trap, its body chilling slowly with death. And a portrait of a man who's been running vigorously up and down stairs with a thermometer in his mouth, so that the photographer can gauge the precise moment to take the second photograph. Other elements in the work may not derive from the camera, but their function is as documentary as a photograph. Two identical plastic water bottles, for example, one of whose liquid contents has been raised by one degree, record this event in the form of differing water levels.

As an exercise in comparative photography, structured around repeated pairs of almost imperceptible visual differences, *Universal Cooling* proposes a radical move away from the photograph as a singular image, to the photograph as a composite representation of the dynamic intervals between things. The photograph is generally understood to encapsulate one discrete moment, to freeze Time in its surface. This, though, is illogical since Time is not singular or stoppable as such: we may structure it pragmatically into hours, minutes, seconds but these are arbitrary divisions, when Time itself is infinitely and forever divisible into ever smaller units. The photograph then, no matter how fast the shutter speed, contains not one but an infinite number of moments. *Dual Workstations (30 seconds late and early)* (1998-99) makes tangible this notion of time summoned through accumulation of clusters of discrete elements. Everything on the left of two seemingly exactly doubled workstations, has come into being exactly 60 seconds before everything in the version on the right. Easy enough to grasp in relation to the clusters of photographs pinned to the wall and buried in the filing cabinets, each divided by a minute from its twin. It is less immediately obvious that the regulation office yuccas have grown from two seeds planted precisely one minute apart, or that the newspapers have been bought one after the other, at a minute's interval. Like *Universal Cooling*, the work resides in the measurable difference between two otherwise imperceptible states.

The newest work in the series takes the subject of motion to add to time and temperature. Again, the piece isolates one measurable phenomenon — one metre of movement in one direction, or, 'a one metre shift of location along the x axis'. This shift in location is documented not from one frontal position but from many — from behind, from above, from below, from different angles. The first freestanding work in the series (the piece takes the form of two rectangular columns appended with paired clusters of images and objects), it represents a kind of advanced 'photographic' cubism in that it melds together not an erratic series of different viewpoints of one object, but a systematic three-dimensional description of a moving space, a shift, between things.
(Kate Bush)

Born in Ulverston, England in 1969. Works in London.

Education
1990-93: Alternative Practice, University of Brighton.
1989-90: Carlisle College of Art.
1984-89: MECS (Mechanical Engineering Craft Studies), Barrow-in-Furness College of Engineering.

Selected solo exhibitions
2002: *Supercollider*, South London Gallery (catalogue). Kunsthalle Zurich (catalogue).
2000: *One of Each*, Galerie Ursula Krinzinger, Vienna (catalogue).
1999: *Keith Tyson*, Delfina, London (catalogue). *Molecular Compound 4*, Kleineshelmhaus, Zurich.
1996: David Zwirner Gallery, New York.
1995: *From the Artmachine*, Anthony Reynolds Gallery, London.

Selected group exhibitions
2002: *Metropolitan Iconography*, São Paulo Bienal.
2001: *Century City, Art and Culture in the Modern Metropolis*, Tate Modern, London (catalogue).
49th Venice Biennale (catalogue).
2nd Berlin Biennale (catalogue).
Nothing, Northern Gallery for Contemporary Art, Sunderland and tour to Contemporary Art Centre, Vilnius and Rooseum, Malmo.
2000: *Dream Machines*, National Touring Exhibition Programme, Hayward Gallery, London; Dundee Contemporary Arts, Scotland (catalogue). *The British Art Show 5*, Edinburgh and UK tour (catalogue). *Over the Edges*, Stedelijk Museum voor Actuele Kunst, Ghent, Belgium (catalogue).
1998: *Seeing Time: Selection from the Pamela and Richard Kramlich Collection of Media Art*, San Francisco Museum of Modern Art (catalogue).
1997: *Private Face — Urban Space*, Gasworks, Athens; Rethymnon Centre for Contemporary Art, Crete.
1995: *Institute of Cultural Anxiety*, Institute of Contemporary Art, London.

Michelle Williams 72–77

Wet Sunday afternoons spent watching vintage and experimental films, especially Michael Powell and Emeric Pressburger's *Black Narcissus* (1947) and Maya Deren's *Meshes of the Afternoon* (1943-59), clearly had an enormous influence on the young video/film maker Michelle Williams. Whilst still a student at Middlesex University, where she studied printmaking before experimenting with both performance and video, Williams produced two versions of *Sunday Afternoon*: the first on Super VHS edited on analogue and transferred to digital, which had a distinctly documentary feel; the second, in a digital format, featuring two dogs rather than one, which is far more jewel-like and compositionally assured. Ever so slightly slowed down to exaggerate the image and the sound of the dogs' licks, the effect for the viewer slips unnervingly between the fictional and the non-fictional, the seductive and the repellent.

Williams' original inspiration for the second film arose from stories she read in the press about old people found dead in their homes accompanied only by their dog. From mourning their beloved owner, the dog's behaviour quickly degenerated into a primitive desire to devour them. What constitutes primeval desire and how do dogs and humans interact when left unhindered by social constraints?

Assuming the role of both model and cameraman (achieved by using a digital handheld LCD), Williams focuses her disembodied camera lens on the sensuous and tactile qualities of every element (animal, human or vegetable) within the scene. Reflecting her interest in the emotional nuances of domestic spaces, Williams manages to transform a typically suburban 1930s living-room into a glamorous and romantic set. In a film in which every element is subject to a high degree of formal control, an almost fetishistic importance is attached to small details such as the feel of the silk dress and glossy nail varnish, the highly polished finish on the floor and the texture of the dogs' hair, eyes and saliva. With considerable assurance, the animals' 'dance' around the woman's body has been choreographed without any narrative intent, but to suggest a mood of erotic desire.

Experimentation with the formal qualities of the film medium and its capacity to manipulate space and time has preoccupied Williams throughout her short career. In *Maiden's Descent* (2001), Williams explored the female body's relationship to space and architecture, reflecting on a scene from *Meshes of the Afternoon*, where the female protagonist falls helplessly down a narrow staircase.

In her new collaboration *The Glut Salon*, which she is currently working on with the artist Eleanor Pearce, film and video will be only one element in an installation, which will comprise objects (original Edwardian and handmade furniture) as well as live performance.
(Brett Rogers)

Born in London in 1979.
Lives and works in London.

Education
1998-2001: BA Fine Arts,
Middlesex University.

Selected group exhibitions
2002: *Heimlich - Unheimlich*, RMIT Gallery, Melbourne, Australia. *Heavy Petting*, DeOoievaar, Den Haag, Netherlands. *National Review of Live Art*, The Arches, Glasgow, Scotland. *Light Structures*, Tate Britain, London; Arnolfini, Bristol.
2001: *Tranz>Tech*, New Media Biennial, Toronto. *Youthquake*, Gallery W139, Amsterdam. *New Contemporaries*, Camden Arts Centre, London; Northern Gallery for Contemporary Art, Sunderland, England.
2000: *Bang! Notes, recordings and other things*, Standpoint Gallery, London. *Uncut Screening*, Institute of Contemporary Art, London.

Shizuka Yokomizo 30–35

Japanese-born Yokomizo, who has lived and worked in London for the past 13 years, may have drawn on her own experience as an outsider in Britain as the starting point for exploring concepts of intimacy and distance in portraiture.
In 1989, following the completion of a philosophy degree in Japan, Yokomizo arrived in Britain and within a year, began studying sculpture. Shortly after starting her MA at Goldsmiths College in 1994, she switched to photography, attracted by the medium's lack of an historical legacy and by its ability to allow her to explore formal and narrative ideas in a fresh manner.

Beginning with *Lost Narratives* (1994) in which she took Christian iconography as her source material, Yokomizo has worked collaboratively with her subjects to produce images that are intimate and distant at the same time, suggestive of 'a moment you can't enter'. Whilst this first series was self-reflective, a means of solving particular problems she posed for herself at the time, the starting point for her next series, *Light* (1995-97), often referred to as the *Saints* series, was the formal/metaphorical device of light itself, employed as a means of creating a narrative. Choosing friends who possessed the same forename as biblical saints (such as Mary, Jerome, Peter, James), Yokomizo researched a set of exterior and interior locations, all of which were important to her in some way, in which to place her subjects. Playing with notions of time and the qualities of artificial light, her subjects appear to take on the character of modern day 'saints', engulfed by haloes of light or surrounded by reflective auras. Time, trust and intimacy were also crucial elements in *Sleepers* (1997-98) in which she photographed her friends falling asleep at night, waiting until that moment when they lost consciousness and slipped into an involuntary state.

Intimacy was replaced with distance in *Stranger* (1998-2001). Here, Yokomizo began by employing a formal means of communication — a letter — to write to someone she had never met, stating that she would be waiting with her camera outside their window at a particular time (always at night) and would, if they agreed, take their portrait as they looked outside. Such nocturnal voyeurism might recall the obsessions of innumerable early twentieth century photographers such as Brassaï,

Kertesz and Brandt or the 'sleuth' strategies employed by more recent artists like Sophie Calle. In Yokomizo's hands however, the night-time settings become simply another device for suggesting the 'strangeness' of the encounter, whereby the notion of who is the subject and who the object of the encounter, is put to the test. The resulting series of 24 images, covering a range of cities from Hiroshima to New York, Blackpool, Stockholm, Berlin, Paris and London, depicts a disparate range of individuals, linked only by the fact that they are mostly young, casually attired and located within their own domestic space. In choosing how to present themselves to the world, some betray a level of mistrust (an understandable reaction to the surveillance they are encountering), others remain largely impassive, whilst a few adopt a pose of mock defiance.

Although continuing to work in photography, Yokomizo has recently (2001-02) broadened her repertoire to include video. Focusing her attention on a new subject area — the elderly — Yokomizo continues her preoccupation with the known /unknown, the visible/invisible. Positioned within the intimate setting of an elderly person's bedroom, the photographer once again succeeds in insinuating herself into the presence of her subject (even though she is an unnoticed presence in the room) concealing herself behind a screen and her camera, awaiting the moment when the subject awakens into consciousness. Juxtaposed with film she shot whilst diving on to the seabed off the coast of Plymouth, this new work attempts to suggest the 'limbo land' which all humans experience, that hinterland between the inner/outer worlds which ultimately manifests itself in the slippage from life to death.
(Brett Rogers)

Born in Tokyo in 1966.
Lives and works in London.

Education
1993-95: MA Fine Art, Goldsmiths College, London.
1990-93: BA Fine Art, Chelsea College of Art and Design, London.
1989-90: Foundation course, Kent Institute of Art and Design, Canterbury.
1985-89: BA Philosophy, Chuo University, Japan.

Selected solo exhibitions
2002: Museo Arte Contemporanea di Roma. The Approach, London.
2001: *Dear Stranger*, Cohan, Leslie + Browne, New York.
2000: *Dear Stranger*, The Approach, London.

Selected group exhibitions
2001: *The Fantastic Recurrence of Certain Situations*, Sala de Exposiciones del canal de Isabel II, Madrid (catalogue). *Senritsumirai-Futuro Anteriore Arte Attuale Dal Giappone*, Centro per l'Arte Contemporanea Luigi Pecci, Prato, Italy. *Artists today*, Yokohama Civic Art Gallery, Yokohama, Japan.

Bettina von Zwehl 66—71

Beginning with her student experiments using photomicrography to document the biological structure of her own saliva, skin, and blood, von Zwehl has exploited the reductive aesthetics of scientific research to enquire into the nature of photography and the limits of portraiture. From 1998, she began to turn the camera outward, focusing upon external rather than internal portraits, always choosing her subjects carefully from people within her own generation. Her sitters appear anonymous, stripped of all personal details but united by identical posing and subject to the same controlled experiment. The nature of these experiments (the effects of gravity on the body whilst holding one's breath, being awoken in the middle of deep sleep, or subject to rigorous exercise) is largely inconsequential, being merely a means to von Zwehl's real interest: an exploration of the relationship and expectations inherent in the act of portraiture.

By replacing the intimacy and insight which one conventionally expects from portraiture, with something far more objective and rational, von Zwehl's project recalls the nineteenth century's faith in the potential of both science and photography to unravel the mysteries of life. Photography's appropriation of the new 'sciences' of phrenology and physiognomy resulted in bizarre experiments by physicians and amateur photographers to register and objectively record the 'true' nature of human character, from the criminal to the insane. The highly controlled and directed experiments which von Zwehl conducts, mimic the approach of nineteenth century photographers such as Francis Galton or Alphonse Bertillon, the French chief of the Identification Service of the Paris Police. In producing his landmark inventory of over 90,000 Paris recidivists, Bertillon consciously attempted to demonstrate scientific 'rigour' in his portraits, by employing the correct lighting to achieve a systematic neutrality and standardisation of expression across his archive.

Equally important as an influence on von Zwehl's work has been western European painting. The impassivity of all her sitters and the use of various pictorial conventions suggest the importance of early European painting. In *Untitled II* (1999), the symmetrical arrangement of the sitters in front of the formal device of a (window)

ledge, combined with the sombre monochrome backgrounds, evokes the mood and conventions of early Netherlandish and Renaissance portraits. In her new series *Profiles* (2001), the reference to a specific Renaissance source (Piero della Francesca's 1470 diptych of the Duke and Duchess of Montefeltro) is clearly acknowledged. Here however, the couples don't really know each other and are linked only by their stare, which is fixed and reciprocated but from which the viewer is totally excluded. Using a special form of flash, von Zwehl succeeds in producing the effect of metallic sharpness of the silhouette which Renaissance painters sought to achieve in their portrait images, focusing the viewer's attention away from distracting details and towards the individual physiognomy of the subjects.
(Brett Rogers)

Born in Munich, Germany in 1971.
Lives and works in London.

Education
1997-99: MA Fine Art Photography, Royal College of Art, London
1994-97: BA (Hons) Photography, London College of Printing.

Selected solo exhibitions
2002: Victoria Miro Gallery, London.
2000: Lombard Freid Fine Arts, New York. Galleria Laura Pecci, Milan.

Selected group exhibitions
2001: *Chelsea Rising*, Contemporary Art Center, New Orleans, USA.
2000: *Breathless! Photography and Time*, Victoria & Albert Museum, London. *Psycho/Soma*, Lombard Freid Fine Arts, New York. *Identities*, Galerie Rodolphe Janssen, Brussels.
1999: *Modern Times I*, Hasselblad Centre, Gothenburg, Sweden (catalogue). *Grosse Kunstausstellung*, Haus der Kunst, Munich.
1998: *John Kobal Photographic Portrait Award*, National Portrait Gallery, London and UK tour. *Les Anglais vus par les Anglais*, Rencontres Internationales de la Photographie, Arles, France.

Published by the British Council,
Visual Arts. 10 Spring Gardens
London SW1A 2BN

Exhibition curators:
Kate Bush, Senior Programmer,
The Photographers' Gallery, London
Brett Rogers, Head of Exhibitions,
The British Council, Visual Arts
In consultation with Igor Spanjol,
Media Art Curator, Moderna Galerija
Ljubljana Museum of Modern Art,
Slovenia

The British Council, Visual Arts
Assistant curator: Frédérique
Dolivet
International tour organiser:
Katie Boot
Workshop manager: Craig Henderson
Workshop registrar: Dana Andrew
Workshop technicians:
Marcus Alexander, Tony Connor,
Gareth Hughes

The Photographers' Gallery
Director: Paul Wombell
Head of Marketing and Development:
Janette Scott
Development Manager:
Tania Robinson
Communications Manager:
Susanna Lawson
Projects Organiser (Talks
and Events): Lisa Le Feuvre
Projects Organiser (Education):
Janice McLaren
Gallery Manager: Jason Welling

Overseas tour launched in Slovenia
at the Moderna Galerija / Museum of
Modern Art Ljubljana (29 August – 6
October 2002)

Catalogue designed by Spin.
Edited by Frédérique Dolivet
Printed by Specialblue
Distributed in the UK by
Cornerhouse Publications
70 Oxford Street,
Manchester M1 5NH
publications@cornerhouse.org
www.cornerhouse.org

ISBN 0 86355 504 7

Publication © The British Council
2002.
Texts © Kate Bush, Brett Rogers,
Alex Farquharson 2002
Images © the artists 2002

Acknowledgements
The artists and their galleries
(The Approach, Stephen Friedman
Gallery, Kerlin Gallery, Lisson
Gallery, Matt's Gallery, Andrew
Mummery Gallery, Anthony Reynolds
Gallery) as well as the following
individuals: Miriam Amari, Zdenka
Badovinac, Warren Beeby, Jane
Bhoyroo, Steven Bode, Lizzie Carey-
Thomas, Stephen Coates, Jo Cole,
Pilar Corrias, Tim Dawson, Emma
Dexter, Patricia Finegan, Stephen
Friedman, Saffron Garner, Steve
Green, Darragh Hogan, David
Hubbard, Nic Hughes, Robin
Klassnik, Rania Kontos, Declan
Long, Nicolas Logsdail, Jake
Miller, Andrew Mummery, Anthony
Reynolds, Andrea Rose, Ben
Rawlingson Plant, Clare Simpson,
Swapna Tamhane

Photographic credits
All illustrations courtesy of
the artists
12–17: courtesy Lisson Gallery,
London
18–23: courtesy Kerlin Gallery,
Dublin
30–35: courtesy The Approach,
London
42–47: courtesy Andrew Mummery
Gallery, London
60–65: courtesy Collection Anthony
T. Podesta, Washington DC
66–71: courtesy Tim Dawson
Contemporary, London
84–89: courtesy Anthony Reynolds
Gallery, London
90–95: courtesy Stephen Friedman
Gallery, London
90 top and 91 bottom commissioned
by BMW Financial Services Group in
1999 and forms part of the
company's corporate art collection
96–101: courtesy Stephen Friedman
Gallery, London
102–107: courtesy Matt's Gallery,
London